WHEN W  K

Other books by the same author include

FOR CHILDREN
Borka
Trubloff
Mr Gumpy's Outing
Avocado Baby
Granpa
Cloudland
Whaddayamean?
Husherbye
The Magic Bed

FOR ADULTS
England
France
The Time of Your Life

WHEN WE
WERE YOUNG

Compiled and illustrated by
John Burningham

RESEARCH AND INTERVIEWS BY ROSE FOOT

BLOOMSBURY

First published in Great Britain 2004
This paperback edition published 2005

Bloomsbury Publishing Plc, 36 Soho Square, London W1D 3QY

A CIP catalogue record for this book is available from the British Library.

ISBN 0 7475 7663 7
9780747576631

10 9 8 7 6 5 4 3 2 1

Typeset by Palimpsest Book Production Ltd, Polmont, Stirlingshire

Printed in Great Britain by Clays Ltd, St Ives plc

www.bloomsbury.com/johnburningham

Contents

Compiler's Note

When observing children, I sometimes try to imagine what they will be like when they grow up. I often wonder to what extent childhood has shaped us as adults.

Having spent the majority of my working life writing stories and drawing for the young, I thought it was time to compile a book looking into the humour, triumphs, traumas and magic of childhood for adults.

This book contains an extraordinary collection of childhood memories, reminiscences, and experiences from a diverse range of people with very different upbringings. I hope you will enjoy them as much as I did, reading each one as it came in between bouts of drawing.

All the contributors have donated their fees to UNICEF, a sum which has been matched by my publishers, as an advance against a royalty on every copy sold.

I am extremely grateful to all those people who have generously written a piece or have been interviewed for this book, for sharing their childhood memories.

John Burningham,
London, July 2004

ANDREW O'HAGAN

Would Swimmers Wearing Green Bands Please Leave the Pool Now

I spent most of my childhood underwater at the Auchen-harvie Baths. I loved it there, being calm in the chlorine broth, looking up through be-goggled eyes at the white legs of the other swimmers, pleased to know those oxygen-lovers would never conquer the lower depths as I had. In the fabled Scottish summers I would go there first thing in the morning and be the last one to leave the pool. It took cunning, but I worked out how to stay on, turning wrinkled and pink-eyed, forever ready to dive down once again to some imagined kingdom below.

A man wearing white shorts sat on a high umpire's stool making sure nobody went too far in any direction, and now and then he would have to take down the big hook off the wall to save the life of some dive-bombed toddler flailing in the middle and taking in water. Bad behaviour was heavily prohibited at the baths but there was no stopping the major-ity, and some days the place became a sort of aquatic Bedlam, with a multitude of hysterical actions going on above and below the surface. An illustrated list of crimes was pinned at five-yard distances round the walls, and we knew them better than we knew the Ten Commandments.

No Smoking
No Bombing
No Petting
No Eating
No Running
No Shouting
No Ducking
No Acrobatics
No Pushing
No Splashing

No Petting? Most of us were at an age where the thought of 'petting' made us fall causally into a coma, so the poster of crimes came to be portentous as well as funny. Kids would scream with pride when they managed to invent a crime that wasn't on the poster, like swearing underwater or peeing in the baby pool.

Crime is often companionable, but when I think of the Auchenharvie Baths I really think of solitude. It was one of the few places in my life where I found it truly possible to be a child: my imagination went unchecked, and I taught myself how to sit on the bottom of the pool, waving my arms for balance, the distant sounds like echoes that couldn't penetrate the world I had made down there. I felt like the sultan of the seven seas, unreachable, defiant, before reluctantly travelling upwards after exactly one minute and five seconds (my personal best) to rejoin the world of instant noise and air and umpires watching the clock.

The only lure was the cafeteria. They had a machine in there that would give you good stuff if you put the right coins in and pressed the right buttons: Caramac bars (F6), curry-flavoured crisps (F11), a roll-and-sausage (F10). The latter could be heated to a gaseous puffy mess in the adjacent microwave oven, the first of its kind I'd ever seen.

I hated leaving the pool – it seemed a bit of an imposition suddenly to have to walk on carpets and pavements when the water had seemed so accommodating. The days were long and at the end I'd look out of the window of the cafeteria at the Scottish clouds and begin to prepare myself for the journey home. The clouds could promise a second dousing, and drops of water to oil the tongue. All the better to speak your excuses for being so late and smiling and unsorry.

First Memories

The first thing I remember is sitting in a pram at the top of a hill with a dead dog lying at my feet.

GRAHAM GREENE, *A Sort of Life* (1971)

Difficult to know what one's first memory is. I remember distinctly my third birthday. The sense of my own importance surges up in me. We are having tea in the garden – in the part of the garden where, later, a hammock swings between two trees.

There is a tea table and it is covered with cakes, with my birthday cake, all sugar icing and with candles in the middle of it. Three candles. And then the exciting occurrence – a tiny red spider, so small that I can hardly see it, runs across the white cloth. And my mother says: 'It's a lucky spider, Agatha, a lucky spider for your birthday . . .' And then the memory fades . . .

AGATHA CHRISTIE, *Autobiography* (1977)

It was on a bright day of midwinter, in New York. The little girl who eventually became me, but as yet was neither me nor anybody else in particular, but that merely a soft anonymous morsel of humanity – this little girl, who bore my name, was going for a walk with her father. The episode is literally the first thing I can remember about her, and therefore I date the birth of her identity from that day.

EDITH WHARTON, *A Backward Glance* (1934)

When does one first begin to remember? When do the waving lights and shadows of dawning consciousness cast their print upon the mind of a child? My earliest memories are of Ireland . . . My nurse, Mrs Everest, was nervous about the Fenians. I gathered these were wicked people and there was no end to what they would do if they had their way. On one occasion when I was out riding on my donkey, we thought we saw a long dark procession of Fenians approaching. I am sure now it must have been the Rifle Brigade out for a route march. But we were all very much alarmed, particularly the donkey, who expressed his anxiety by kicking. I was thrown off and had concussion of the brain. This was my first introduction to Irish politics!

WINSTON CHURCHILL, *My Early Life* (1930)

But the memories that seem important to remember are not of these chance touchings of the skirts of history, but of quite simple things, drifting snowflakes seen through a melted peephole in a frosted nursery window, the sun like a red-hot penny in the smoky Leeds sky, and the dreadful screaming of a wounded hare. That last I can never forget.

ARTHUR RANSOME, *The Autobiography of Arthur Ransome* (1976)

I have an impression on my mind, which I cannot distinguish from actual remembrance, of the touch of Peggoty's forefinger as she used to hold it out to me, and of its being roughened by needlework like a pocket nutmeg-grater.

This may be fancy, though I think the memory of most of us can go farther back into such times than many of us suppose; just as I believe the power of observation in numbers of very young children to be quite wonderful for its closeness and accuracy. Indeed, I think that most grown men who are remarkable in this respect, may with greater propriety be said not to have lost the faculty than to have acquired it; the rather, as I generally observe such men to retain a certain freshness, and gentleness, and capacity of being pleased, which are also an inheritance they have preserved from their childhood.

CHARLES DICKENS, *David Copperfield* (1849–50)

PATRICIA HODGE

I realise that the possession of a great memory is a professional advantage. Privately, it has endowed me with a myriad of snapshots that even go back to toddler-hood, and are alarmingly vivid:

Standing up in my cot and watching my father shave while he sang 'Put another nickel in/In the nickelodeon'. (That dates me.)

Amusing myself by tipping an entire box of my mother's face powder over the bed, to get a better look.

Getting imprisoned, in the side passage of my home, by the neighbour's cat who sat leering at me from the wall with such menace that I dared not run past. I was sure he had murder in mind, and I must have been stuck there for ages hearing my frantic parents' voices calling for me.

Then there are the roots of my love affair with the theatre which began, not unusually, with pantomime. I so believed in what I was watching, that in my mind Jack and Jill actually walked out from the painted backdrop.

For years, this love affair was sustained by the only local facility open to me, namely the Cleethorpes Pier, where the highlight of the year was the East Coast Dance Festival. It was finally confirmed when I saw professional theatre for the first time, at the age of ten, in the shape of *Where the Rainbow Ends* at the Victoria Palace. I have never recovered.

My earliest memory of learning a text is from nursery school. We were bidden to recite, daily:

> Gentle Jesus, meek and mild,
> Look upon a little child.
> Pity my simplicity,
> Suffer me to come to thee.

I spent a great deal of time worrying myself silly about those poor mice, and what on earth they were doing in that awful place called Plicity.

Dreams

When I was five the black dreams came;
Nothing after was quite the same.

LOUIS MACNEICE, 'Autobiography' (1940)

My bad dreams were of two kinds, those about spectres and those about insects. The second were, beyond comparison, the worse; to this day I would rather meet a ghost than a tarantula. And to this day I could almost find it in my heart to rationalise and justify my phobia. As Owen Barfield once said to me, 'The trouble about insects is that they are like French loco-motives – they have all the works on the outside.' The works – that is the trouble. Their angular limbs, their jerky movements, their dry metallic noises, all suggest either machines that have come to life or life degenerating into mechanism. You may add that in the hive and the ant-hill we see fully realised the two things some of us most dread for our own species – the dominance of the female and the dominance of the collective.

C. S. LEWIS, *Surprised by Joy* (1955)

Children brought up in nicely kept houses where spiders are not tolerated, are afraid of spiders, and in many cases this fear clings to them when they have become grown. I have never seen peasants, whether man, woman, or child, who were afraid of spiders.

J. J. ROUSSEAU, *Emile or Treatise on Education* (1824)

SEAMUS HEANEY

An Iridescence

I was late on the scene. What I remember are smashed bushes
and cut up ground, the bark skinned off the thorn trees and
bits of tramped down chocolate everywhere. Rain had fallen,
adding melancholy to the mystery. It was only a hole in the
hedge but it could have been an entrance to the underworld.
When I came to recall it in a sonnet, I wanted to keep the
actuality of Cadbury's 'trademark purple', although the scene
had the aura of a place where (in the words of Patrick
Kavanagh) 'some strange thing had happened'.

A chocolate van had crashed. That was the news.
Had skidded off the road at Duggan's Hill.
That night the bedtime cocoa had a smell
Of leaf-mould off it and through Duggan's trees
Deep-shining in the polished windowless
Side sheeting of that lumbered vehicle
A moon made headway in the trademark purple,
Made ground light of foil wrappings and smashed glass
And sowed the iris murk with marigold.
All that was left next day was a ruined hedge,
Mould and raw verges where a crane had pulled
The van free through an iridescent sludge,
Floatings on it of spoils from the wrecked load
And a trail of silver papers up the road.

He had taken me aside one day, and promised me a silver fourpenny on the first of every month if I would only keep my 'weather-eye open for a seafaring man with one leg' and let him know the moment he came . . .

How that personage haunted my dreams, I need scarcely tell you. On stormy nights, when the wind shook the four corners of the house, and the surf roared along the cove and up the cliffs, I would see him in a thousand forms, and with a

thousand diabolical expressions. Now the leg would be cut off at the knee, now at the hip; now he was a monstrous kind of creature who had never had but the one leg, and that in the middle of his body. To see him leap and run and pursue me over hedge and ditch was the worst of nightmares. And altogether I paid pretty dear for my monthly fourpenny piece in the shape of these abominable fancies.

R. L. STEVENSON, *Treasure Island* (1883)

Schooldays

'Can you do Addition?' the White Queen asked. 'What's one and one and one and one and one and one and one and one and one and one?'

'I don't know,' said Alice. 'I lost count.'

LEWIS CARROLL, *Through the Looking-Glass* (1887)

When, after the examinations at the end of the first term, she looked at the papers they had been set, she read some of the more vulnerable of the questions aloud with the greatest contempt: 'A window cleaner carries a uniform 60-lb. ladder 15 ft. long, at one end of which a bucket of water weighing 40 lb. is hung. At what point must he support the ladder to carry it horizontally? Where is the c.g. of his load?' Miss Brodie looked at the paper, after reading out this question as if to indicate that she could not believe her eyes. Many a time she gave the girls to understand that the solution to such problems would be quite useless to Sybil Thorndike, Anna Pavlova and the late Helen of Troy.

MURIEL SPARK, *The Prime of Miss Jean Brodie* (1961)

ASSOCIATED EXAMINING BOARD

for the General Certificate of Education

Summer Examination, 1955
Ordinary Level

MATHEMATICS
Paper I

Monday, June 13th, 9.30 to 11.30 a.m.
(Two hours allowed)

SECTION A.

Answer **all** *questions in this section.*

A. 1. (a) Find the value of $3 \cdot 14 \, (5 \cdot 3^2 - 4 \cdot 7^2)$.

(b) If $\dfrac{1}{v} - \dfrac{1}{u} = \dfrac{1}{f}$, find f when $u = 12 \cdot 5$ and $v = 7 \cdot 5$.

(c) An equilateral triangle ABX is described on the side AB of a square $ABCD$ and outside the square. Calculate the angles of the triangle XBD.

A. 2. (a) Copper is bought at £350 per ton and sold at £22 15s. 0d. per cwt. Calculate the percentage profit on the cost price.

(b) The area of a trapezium is given by the formula

$$A = \frac{a + b}{2} \cdot h.$$

Express b in terms of A, a and h.

(c) If $\tan A = \dfrac{5}{12}$ and A is an acute angle, find $\cos A$ and $\sin (180° - A)$ without using tables.

[*Turn over*

A. 3. (a) A map is drawn to a scale of 10 cm to 1 km. Calculate:

    (i) the length on the map of a line which represents 950 cm;

    (ii) the length on the map of the side of a square which represents an area of 2·25 sq. km.

(b) In an ironmonger's shop a man bought m lb of rivets at p shillings a lb; in a second shop he bought n lb of similar rivets at q shillings a lb. What was the average price in shillings per lb paid for the rivets?

How many pounds of rivets could be bought for £1 at this average price?

A. 4. (a) Solve the equation

$$\frac{t-1}{4} - \frac{3t-1}{5} = 1.$$

(b) Fig. 1 shows a vertical cross-section of a cylinder, centre C, and radius 2·5 cm, fitting into a V-shaped groove.

Calculate VB given that $VT = 6$ cm.

Calculate also the angle TVS of the groove.

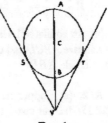

Fig. 1

A. 5. (a) Fig. 2 shows a lamp A, 21 ft above the ground. It casts a shadow CM, 10 ft long, of a man MN, 6 ft tall. Calculate the horizontal distance MB of the man from the lamp.

(b) A triangular plate ABC is to be made in which $AB = 8$ in., $AC = 5$ in. and the angle $BAC = 43°$. Calculate the length of BC, correct to the nearest $\frac{1}{16}''$.

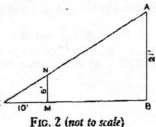

Fig. 2 (*not to scale*)

Even when the lessons are done, the worst is yet to happen, in the shape of an appalling sum. This is invented for me, and delivered to me orally by Mr Murdstone, and begins, 'If I go into a cheesemonger's shop, and buy five thousand double-Gloucester cheeses at fourpence halfpenny each, present payment' – at which I see Miss Murdstone secretly overjoyed. I pore over these cheeses without any result or enlightenment until dinner time; when, having made a mulatto of myself by getting the dirt of the slate into the pores of my skin, I have a slice of bread to help me out with the cheeses, and am considered in disgrace for the rest of the evening.

CHARLES DICKENS, *David Copperfield* (1849–50)

I never knew how many apples a farmer had left in his basket if he gave his wife two-thirds. Or how much water slipped away in an hour if the bath-plug was released and the tap dripped at the rate of fifty drops per minute. What the Hell! I was lost.

DIRK BOGARDE, *A Postillion Struck by Lightning* (1977)

Shall I venture to state, at this point, the most important, the most useful rule of all education? It is not to gain time, but to lose it.

J. J. ROUSSEAU, *Emile or Treatise on Education* (1824)

It was not we who were driven mad by such subjects as mental arithmetic, but the teachers. One of them, a small, knock-kneed man who we nicknamed 'Bandy', used to collapse impotently across his desk at the answers received to such problems of a man and a half who ate a cake and a half in a day and a half. He would cover his eyes with his hands and moan 'Donkeys', then bawl glaring, 'Thick-headed, good-for-nothing idiots', and cover his eyes again.

WALTER GREENWOOD, *The Old School*, ed. Graham Greene (1934)

KOFI ANNAN

At times in life, it's not other people or events beyond your control that hold you back or get in the way. Your own attitude can be just as big a problem.

At school in Ghana, Africa, I was one of a group of boys who sat on the floor of our professor's office for a weekly lesson in 'spoken English'. One day, the professor put a large sheet of white paper on the wall. The paper had a little black dot on the right-hand corner. When the professor asked, 'Boys, what do you see?' we all shouted together: 'A black dot!' The professor stepped back and said, 'So, not a single one of you saw the white sheet of paper. You only saw the black dot. This is the awful thing about human nature. People never see the goodness of things and the broader picture. Don't go through life with that attitude.'

Life teaches you lessons in surprising ways and when you least expect it. One of the most important lessons I ever learned came from a sheet of paper and a black dot. They may seem like small things, but they were enough to prompt big changes in my outlook on life.

First Day

When the last sound of my mother's departing wheels had died away, the Headmaster invited me to hand over any money I had in my possession. I produced my three half-crowns, which were duly entered in a book, and I was told that from time to time there would be a 'shop' at the school with all sorts of things which one would like to have and that I could choose what I liked up to the limit of the seven and sixpence. Then we quitted the Headmaster's parlour and the comfortable private side of the house, and entered the more bleak apartments reserved for the instruction and accommodation of the pupils. I was taken into a Form Room and told to sit at a desk. All the other boys were out of doors, and I was alone with the Form Master. He produced a thin greeny-brown, covered book filled with words in different types of print.

'You have never done any Latin before, have you?' he said.

'No, sir.'

'This is a Latin grammar.' He opened it at a well-thumbed page. 'You must learn this,' he said, pointing to a number of words in a frame of lines. 'I will come back in half an hour and see what you know.'

Behold me then on a gloomy evening, with an aching heart, seated in front of the First Declension.

WINSTON CHURCHILL, *My Early Life* (1930)

Latin is a subject
That no one enjoys;
It killed the ancient Romans
And now it is killing boys.
ANON.

The schoolhouse consisted of a single room, with a Western-style roof, on the other side of the hill from Qunu. I was seven years old, and on the day before I was to begin, my father took me aside and told me that I must be dressed properly for school. Until that time I, like all the other boys in Qunu, had worn only a blanket, which was wrapped round one shoulder and pinned at the waist. My father took a pair of his trousers and cut them at the knee. He told me to put them on, which I did, and they were roughly the correct length, although the waist was far too large. My father then took a piece of string and drew the trousers in at the waist. I must have been a comical sight, but I have never owned a suit I was prouder to wear than my father's cut-off trousers.

On the first day of school my teacher, Miss Mdingane, gave each of us an English name and said that thenceforth that was the name we would answer to in school. This was the custom among Africans in those days and was undoubtedly due to the British bias in our education. The education I received was a British education, in which British ideas, British culture and British institutions were automatically assumed to be superior. There was no such thing as African culture.

Africans of my generation – and even today – generally have both a Western and an African name. Whites were unable or unwilling to pronounce an African name, and considered it uncivilised to have one.

That day, Miss Mdingane told me that my new name was Nelson. Why she bestowed this particular name upon me I have no idea. Perhaps it had something to do with the great British sea captain Lord Nelson, but that would be only a guess.

NELSON MANDELA, *Long Walk to Freedom* (1994)

Usually at the end of the lesson a certain limerick was asked for and granted, the point of the performance being that the word 'screamed' in it was to be involuntarily enacted by oneself every time Mr Burness gave a formidable squeeze to the hand he held in his beefy paw as he recited the lines:

There was a young lady from Russia
Who (squeeze) whenever you'd crush her.
She (squeeze) and she (squeeze) . . .

by which time the pain would have become so excruciating that we never got any farther.

VLADIMIR NABOKOV, *Speak, Memory* (1967)

Often and often afterwards, the beloved Aunt would ask me why I had never told any one how I was being treated. Children tell little more than animals, for what comes to them they accept as eternally established. Also badly-treated children have a clear notion of what they are likely to get if they betray the secrets of a prison-house before they are clear of it.

RUDYARD KIPLING, *Something of Myself* (1937)

Mount Stephen House,
Field, B.C. Canada
October 12, 1907

Dear Sir – My esteemed Son – O John, etc.

We reached this place last night and found your first letter from school waiting for us. It had been sent on from Montreal. You can just imagine how delighted we were to get it and how we read it over and over again.

I am very pleased to know that you like school – I feel sure that you will like it more and more as time goes on and you settle down and make your own friends. But I know exactly how homesick you feel at first. I can remember how I felt when I first went to school at Westward Ho! But my school was more than two hundred miles from my home – my Father and Mother were in India and I knew that I should not see them for years. The school was more than two hundred boys of all ages from eighteen to twelve. I was nearly the youngest – and the grub was simply beastly.

Now with you, you are not thirty miles from home – you are by no means the youngest chap here – and they look after you in a way that no one ever dreamed of doing when I was young . . .

Well, from all I can discover, you behaved yourself like a man when you felt homesick. I understand that you did not flop about and blub and whine but carried on quietly. Good man! Next time it will come easier to you to keep control over yourself and the time after that easier still . . .

RUDYARD KIPLING, *O Beloved Kids*, ed. Elliot Gilbert (1983)

It's true that some Gypsy girls are brought up to cook and clean the house and get married, and some boys are brought up to go round collecting scrap metal to bring money into the home, but I was brought up to believe that I could do anything I want to do. Neither my dad nor my uncles can read or write, and all my family are very proud of what I've achieved at school.

DEAN VINE, 'Gypsy Voices', *Guardian* (19 August 2003)

Their dream, and this went on quite far into my professional life, was that I would be the best at music school but not quite good enough for a concert career. I would then go back to Japan, live with them, teach piano and make a lot of money, because it can be very lucrative. And I'd play one recital a year where they could turn up with great pride and people would say 'Mr Uchida, aren't you lucky with your daughter?'

MITSUKO UCHIDA, *Guardian* (21 December 2002)

I would rather Summerhill produced a happy street sweeper than a neurotic prime minister.

A. S. NEILL, Headmaster of Summerhill

I can still see the terrible Abbot Régnier, who was nicknamed 'spider of the night'. His favourite punishment was to gather together all the naughty little boys beneath his big black cape and keep them there throughout the school break. When the bell rang he would open up his cape and scream at us: 'Lavatory!' And we'd all rush to the toilets.

HENRI CARTIER-BRESSON, *Le Monde* (23 August 2002)

. . . For some reason or other, a boy often does pass, from an early stage when he wants to know nearly everything, to a later stage when he wants to know next to nothing.

G. K. CHESTERTON, *Autobiography* (1936)

Mr Polly went into the National School at six, and he left the private school at fourteen, and by that time his mind was in much the same state that you would be in, dear reader, if you were operated upon for appendicitis by a well-meaning, boldly enterprising, but rather overworked and underpaid butcher boy, who was superseded towards the climax of the operation by a left-handed clerk of high principles but intemperate habits – that is to say, it was in a thorough mess. The nice little curiosities and willingness of a child were in a jumbled and thwarted condition, hacked and cut about – the operators had left, so to speak, all their sponges and ligatures in the mangled confusion – and Mr Polly had lost much of his natural confidence, so far as figures and sciences and languages and the possibilities of learning things were concerned. He thought of the present world no longer as a wonderland of experiences, but as geography and history, as the repeating of names that were hard to pronounce, and lists of products and populations and heights and lengths, and as lists and dates – oh! And Boredom indescribable.

H. G. WELLS, *The History of Mr Polly* (1910)

Geography had been one of his strong points. He was aware of the rivers of Asia in their order, and of the principal products of Uruguay; and he could name the capitals of nearly all the United States. But he had never been instructed for five minutes in the geography of his native country, of which he knew neither the boundaries nor the rivers nor the terrene characteristics. He could have drawn a map of the Orinoco, but he could not have found the Trent in a day's march; he did not even know where his drinking-water came from.

ARNOLD BENNETT, *Clayhanger* (1910)

Correspondence courses still arrived by every post, but she wondered what she was paying money for when she could do better herself. She taught us geography by sloshing water into our sand pit and making continents, isthmuses, estuaries, islands. Being taught to see land masses and oceans like this repeats that stage of human knowledge when the world was flat. Then she ordered a little globe from Salisbury which arrived on the train, and with it we entered the mind of Copernicus. She sat my father in his folding chair on the sharp slope down outside the house, summoned the cook and the piccanin from the kitchen. My father was the sun. The two servants were the heavy planets, Jupiter and Saturn. Stones stood for Pluto, for Mars. I was Mercury and my brother Venus, running around my father, while she was the earth, moving slowly. 'You have to imagine the stars are moving at different rates, everything moving, all the time.' And then she abolished this system of cosmic order with an impatient wave of her hand.

DORIS LESSING, *Under My Skin* (1994)

From the letters of James Milnes Gaskell, a boy at Eton

Eton, May 7th 1824

My dearest Mama,

...A fellow of the name of Morrell sleeps in the room next to mine; and makes furious noises whether he wants the maid or not. 'Betsy,' balls he, 'Betsy, hoi, Betsy,' stamping and kicking etc ...

May 8th

My dearest Mama,

...Morrell is now in my room with another boy; he is cutting holes in and completely spoiling my table. He seized my knife and made very large gashes in the ceiling and paper of my room. I hope that I have temper enough not to mind their insulting me in every possible kind of way, but to hear the very worst species of uncontrolled swearing and particularly directed against me, because I do not understand the scandalous words of which they alone know the meaning ...

May 10th

My dearest Mother,

...Yesterday several of the boys followed me about, crying out; 'What! Do you never swear?' Upon answering in the negative on the ground that it was decidedly wrong, they said 'What a sap!'; and for this reason I was assailed with hisses on entering the school room today ... Notwithstanding all the care which it was possible for me to use, they have been in my room, seized one of my knives and snuffers, and I despair of ever recovering them. When I had gone to bed, Trench came into my room, swearing and pulled me about in every sort of way he could think of. One of them has also broken about 5 panes of glass in my window, and this is chiefly to be attributed to my not swearing with them. The more cold and quiet I am, the more am I hooted about the school . . .

May 11th
My darling Mother,
    . . . I must ask your advice about Trench's conduct. He is very strong, blustering and rough, and he came into my room yesterday and tore my verses on 'Magic' to pieces . . .

May 13th
My dearest Mama,
    . . . My poor hat has suffered in the wars, for Halifax and Morrell have made it their football this morning, and tossed it about most cruelly . . .

May 19th
My dearest Mother,
    I have done my work and can assure you that I have a great many things to tell you. Yesterday evening Trench obliged me to come into his room, where he, Tucker, Boughey and the two Bullocks agreed, as they termed it, to break my head if I was not able to answer to their satisfaction all the questions which were to be put to me. Accordingly I positively refused to answer their questions, as they were of a sort and nature, which it is indeed difficult for anyone to conceive. The consequences of my refusal were, however, somewhat disastrous for though I had not a bloody nose, it was hurt, and I had to the *ne plus ultra* its usual concomitant, a black eye which was hit by a board in the scuffle. This morning too, Trench hit violently

my poor wounded eye, and I have been rubbing it with vinegar, by which means I have been much eased.

This morning was the first time in which I went out of bounds. I went with Bankes ma to dig in his garden. He has hired a very pretty one for 2 pounds a year, full of fruit trees and beautiful flowers, tulips, roses, periwinkles, etc. I have been digging and raking his beds for nearly two hours, and have enjoyed myself very much . . .

Your affecte child, Milzy.

May 22nd

My dearest Mama,

I am sorry to say that my tormentors have not ceased to torment me in the open manner which you speak of. This morning, I confess, I am very sorry that I took my prayer book into Church, for on my return they took it from me by main force and kicked it backwards and forwards through the mud, which has sadly injured it. They were not, however, content with this, but about 6, after having carried their main object of enclosing me in a corner, threw large bricks and stones at me for a considerable time. Two or three hit me, but thank God none on the face; many, however, whizzed close to my head – the smallest were about the size of a half crown and the largest of a common brick, most of them large pieces of the latter. It is wonderful that I have escaped almost unhurt. Both my arms are of the most beautiful mulatto colour with kicks and blows, and I cannot use my left one much. I think how fortunate I have been not to lose an eye. I hope I shall not be disfigured when you come to Eton . . .

Your affecte son, JMG

JAMES MILNES GASKELL, *An Eton Boy*, ed. Charles Milnes Gaskell (1939)

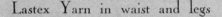

Our uniforms were very uncomfortable, especially the knickers. We had to wear big bloomer-type things. Perhaps that's why I don't wear knickers now!

VIVIENNE WESTWOOD, in *Fashion and Perversity* (1996)

We learnt a little dancing, mainly mazurkas and quadrilles, but in response to the demands of some of the more worldly parents, Reverend Mother reluctantly allowed the elder ones to learn the Valse. It was a rigid affair, that Valse. We danced it, not in silk frocks, but in our clumsy serge uniforms and cotton gloves and thick black stockings and, as in no circumstances were we allowed to encircle each other's waists, each girl held her partner stiffly at arm's length, as, a full yard apart, the couples gyrated slowly round the room.

ANTONIA WHITE, *The Old School*, ed. Graham Greene (1934)

I shall never forget the joy of going to school and the gorgeous smell of the paint I was allowed to use, nor the inspiration and help the Headmistress, Miss McCroben gave me ... My headmistress knew I detested sports and games. I loved dancing, music, drawing and painting. And wonderfully, when all had departed to the playing fields I found myself miraculously alone with easel, paints and paper in the school.

BARBARA HEPWORTH, *A Pictorial Autobiography* (1970)

I can recover still that exasperated sense of being in some way crippled, and I think it was not to do with being unable to draw, but a temporary rage with the condition of childhood. Every now and then, children identify themselves. They see what they are – people at an early stage of development, with all that that implies. And the perception is appalling.

PENELOPE LIVELY, *Oleander, Jacaranda* (1994)

Most of the rules were to do with washing. Not that we should wash, but that we should not. Cleanliness for these women was an invitation to the devil. We were told to wash our hands only to the wrists, keeping sleeves rolled down. Only our faces, with a washcloth soaped thick: if our eyes stung, we must offer the pain to God. We might bathe only once a week. The nuns told us that good children would agree to wear the wooden board that stood always against the bathroom wall, when we bathed. The board had a hole in it for the head, and was designed to rest on the sides of the bath, making it impossible to see our bodies. But no one would.

DORIS LESSING, *Under My Skin* (1994)

Tuck-Box

A tuck-box is a small pinewood trunk which is very strongly made, and no boy has ever gone as a boarder to an English Prep School without one. It is his own secret store-house, as secret as a lady's handbag, and there is an unwritten law that no other boy, no teacher, not even the Headmaster himself has the right to pry into the contents of your tuck-box. The owner has a key in his pocket and that is where it stays. At St Peter's, the tuck-boxes were ranged shoulder to shoulder all around the four walls of the changing-room and your own tuck-box stood directly below the peg on which you hung your games clothes. A tuck-box, as the name implies, is a box in which you store your tuck. At Prep School in those days, a parcel of tuck was sent once a week by anxious mothers to their ravenous little sons, and an average tuck-box would probably contain, at almost any time, half a home-made currant cake, a packet of squashed-fly biscuits, a couple of oranges, an apple, a banana, a pot of strawberry jam or Marmite, a bar of chocolate, a bag of Liquorice Allsorts and a tin of Bassett's lemonade powder. An English school in those days was purely a money-making business owned and operated by the Headmaster. It suited him, therefore, to give the boys as little food as possible himself and to encourage the parents in various cunning ways to feed their offspring by parcel-post from home.

'By all means, my dear Mrs Dahl, *do* send your boy some little treats now and again,' he would say. 'Perhaps a few oranges and apples once a week' – fruit was very expensive – 'and a nice currant cake, a *large* currant cake perhaps because small boys have large appetites do they not, ha-ha-ha . . . Yes,

yes, as *often* as you like. *More* than once a week if you wish ...
Of *course* he'll be getting plenty of good food here, the best
there is, but it never tastes *quite* the same as home cooking,
does it? I'm sure you wouldn't want him to be the only one
who doesn't get a lovely parcel from home every week.'

As well as tuck, a tuck-box would also contain all manner
of treasures such as a magnet, a pocket-knife, a compass, a ball
of string, a clockwork racing-car, half a dozen lead soldiers, a
box of conjuring tricks, some tiddly-winks, a Mexican jumping bean, a catapult, some foreign stamps, a couple of stink-
bombs, and I remember one boy called Arkle who drilled an
airhole in the lid of his tuck-box and kept a pet frog in there
which he fed on slugs.

ROALD DAHL, *Boy* (1984)

Carrot Top

'Have you ever seen such hair! It's a real flaming bonfire! And what shoes!' Bengt continued. 'Couldn't I please borrow one of them? I'd like to go for a row, and I haven't got a boat.'

Then he took hold of one of Pippi's pigtails, but quickly dropped it and said, 'Ouch! I burned myself!'

The five boys made a ring round Pippi and hopped about and yelled, 'Carrot top! Carrot top!'

Pippi stood in the middle of the ring and smiled in a friendly manner. Bengt had hoped she would become angry or begin to cry. At the very least she ought to look scared. When nothing else worked, he pushed her.

'I don't think you have particularly good manners with ladies,' said Pippi. Then she lifted him high into the air with her strong arms. She carried him to a nearby birch tree, and hung him across a branch. Then she took the next boy and hung him on another branch. And then she took the next one and sat him on the high gatepost outside the house, and then she took the *next* one and threw him right over the fence, leaving him sitting in a bed of flowers in the next-door garden. She put the last of the bullies into a little toy cart that stood on the road . . . and the bullies were quite speechless with astonishment.

ASTRID LINDGREN, *Pippi Longstocking* (1954)

A friend who was put to work on the Burma railway once told me that he was greeted, on arrival, by a fellow prisoner-of-war who said, 'Cheer up. It's not half as bad as Marlborough.'

JOHN MORTIMER, *Clinging to the Wreckage* (1982)

I have known Oldie enter the schoolroom after breakfast, cast his eyes round, and remark, 'Oh there you are, Rees, you horrid boy. If I'm not too tired I shall give you a good drubbing this afternoon.' He was not angry, nor was he joking. He was a big, bearded man with full lips like an Assyrian king on a monument, immensely strong, physically dirty. Everyone talks of sadism nowadays but I question whether his cruelty had any erotic element in it. I half divined then, and seem to see clearly now, what all his whipping-boys had in common. They were the boys who fell below a certain social status, the boys with vulgar accents. Poor P — dear, honest, hard-working, friendly,

healthily pious P – was flogged incessantly, I now think, for one offence only; he was the son of a dentist. I have seen Oldie make that child bend down at one end of the schoolroom and then take a run of the room's length at each stroke; but P was the trained sufferer of countless thrashings and no sound escaped him until, towards the end of the torture, there came a noise quite unlike a human utterance. That peculiar croaking or rattling cry, that, and the grey faces of all the other boys, and their deathlike stillness, are among the memories I could willingly dispense with.

C. S. LEWIS, *Surprised by Joy* (1955)

It was not a very good example of running away. I did not run away romantically, to join a ship and go to sea. I did not run to seek a refuge among friends, for I had none within reach. I did not try to go home, or even to my dear great-aunt for, much as I loved her, I knew very well that in the matter of running away not even she would be on my side. I merely ran away, without any thought of destination. I ran away over the Kirkstone Pass, taking the turn to the right off the Windermere–Ambleside road, trudging blindly through the Troutbeck valley, climbing up and up the steep, winding road and at last, very tired, passing at the summit of the pass the Traveller's Rest, no rest for me, the old inn that claims to be the highest in England, and so on and down the other side between the enormous hills into country I had never seen. My only idea was to keep going. Tired right out, I was still trudging like a machine when my running away was brought to an end by the sight of a coach climbing up towards the pass from Ullswater. Hitherto, at sight or sound of other people, I had slipped off the road and hidden till they went by. Here there was no bracken in which to hide, no trees, and I was too tired to do anything but keep on walking. The coach moving slowly up the steep came to meet me. A shout came from the red-coated driver on the box-seat. It was my friend Red Coat Robinson. He asked me where I was away to and I could not tell him because I did not know. 'Tha'd better climb oop here, lad,' he said, making room for me beside him, and I had not the strength to refuse. My running away was over and I came back to Windermere on the box-seat of the Ullswater coach.

ARTHUR RANSOME, *The Autobiography of Arthur Ransome* (1976)

The bus served three schools. The secondary modern (mixed), the boys' grammar school and the girls' high school, and it had an elaborate unspoken seating plan.

The back seats were reserved for big girls of fourteen and fifteen who went to the secondary modern, but only just. They had perms, boyfriends and jobs lined up, and they wore their school uniforms in a sketchy, customised way, with extra bits and bits missing, and nylons whose ladders they fixed showily with nail varnish. They had a lot to talk about and laugh over in private. They painted their nails on the way home and picked off the varnish the next morning, although sometimes they passed round a bottle of remover that smelled headily of pear-drops. They didn't have homework, but kept changes of clothes in shopping bags they used for satchels; school was for them a last concession to other people's picture of childhood, for in the country girls were grown up at fifteen.

The secondary modern boys were younger for their age and scuffled about in the middle seats, playing at being wild, priding themselves on the filthiness of their ties and wearing spare cigarettes behind their ears. Although they sometimes looked up girls' skirts and told dirty jokes, they were second-class passengers, the bus was girl territory, the real tearaways among the boys didn't stoop to catch the bus, but biked to school on the days they weren't truanting.

And the grammar school boys and high school girls, a conspicuous and shifty minority, distributed themselves around the front seats as they boarded. Grammar school boys stood out sacrificially in bright purple blazers and caps. At least the high school's navy blue matched the majority – although only at a distance, there was no getting round the stigma. The very

first time I caught the bus I committed the terrible solecism of sitting next to a big girl who was saving a seat for her friend in the next-to-back row. She very soon – with a kind of matronly contempt – let me know my mistake. Those first few months I ended up more often than not next to a real pariah, Gilbert, a pale and soft-spoken grammar school boy whose mother had once complained to the bus driver when a rude boy stole his cap. In any case, sitting next to someone of the opposite sex meant you were nobody.

In theory we who'd passed the eleven-plus were supposed to despise the secondary modern kids for being common and thick. In practice we envied them for knowing how to be outsiders and as we grew older we aped their style: caps and berets balled up in pockets, greased and lacquered quiffs of hair, secret lockets and chains and rings on them under their shirts.

When rock and roll and rebels without a cause hit Whitchurch they were ready with the right look and so were we. In time my old Hammer school enemy Gail and I would even form our own girl gang and inherit the back seat. But for now being bussed just felt very lonely. In my oversized gabardine raincoat (with hood), over the top of my cardboard stiff blazer, over the top of my oversized gymslip, with my new beret and badge and my imitation-leather satchel weighed down that first morning with my shoe bag and plimsoles and indoor sandals, all marked with my name in indelible ink as instructed, I was like an evacuee or a displaced person.

LORNA SAGE, *Bad Blood* (2000)

I cannot remember whether it was that very night that I wet-ted my bed again, but at any rate I did wet it again quite soon. Oh, the despair, the feeling of cruel injustice, after all my prayers and resolutions, at once again waking between the clammy sheets! There was no chance of hiding what I had done. The grim statuesque matron, Margaret by name, arrived in the dormitory specially to inspect my bed. She pulled back the clothes, then drew herself up, and the dreaded words seemed to come rolling out of her like a peal of thunder:

'REPORT YOURSELF to the Headmaster after breakfast!' I put REPORT YOURSELF in capitals because that was how it appeared in my mind. I do not know how many times I heard that phrase during my early years at St Cyprian's. It was only very rarely that it did not mean a beating. The words always had a portentous sound in my ears, like muffled drums or the words of the death sentence.

GEORGE ORWELL, *Partisan Review* (1952)

This time tomorrow where shall I be?
Not in this academy,
No more Latin, no more French,
Nor more sitting on a hard school bench;
No more beetles in my tea
Making googly eyes at me;
No more spiders in my bath
Trying hard to make me laugh
No more slugs in my dinner
Which the staff say make me thinner.
When the train goes puff, puff, puff.
I'll be in it sure enough.

ANON.

My last memory is the headmaster's parting shot: 'Well, good-bye, Graves, and remember that your best friend is the waste-paper basket.' This has proved good advice, though not perhaps in the sense he intended: few writers seem to send their work through as many drafts as I do.

ROBERT GRAVES, *Goodbye to All That* (1929)

JUNG CHANG

In 1964, I was twelve. That year Chairman Mao denounced cultivating flowers and grass as 'feudal' and 'bourgeois', and ordered 'Get rid of most gardeners'. So I had to go out with my fellow pupils to remove the grass from the school lawn. I was very sad because instinctively I loved flowers and grass but I could not express my real feelings. Like all children across China, I had been taught to examine my thoughts and to criticise myself for harbouring any instincts that went against Mao's instructions. We had been brought up to regard Mao as our God. As children, if we wanted to convince someone of the absolute truth we would say, 'I swear to Chairman Mao'.

My secondary school was the oldest public (not private) school in China. It was founded in 141 BC. There was a big temple devoted to Confucius, the synonym of Chinese culture. The grounds were huge, with many gardens, and the hill behind the temple was a mass of plants. When I was at that school, my ambition was to become a horticulturist, inspired by the beautiful gardens.

The lawn was between the temple and the school building, beside some basketball courts. Before Mao's order, we used to spend our lunch breaks sitting on the grass and enjoying the sun if it was shining. All around were peach trees and plum trees which in spring were a sea of pink and white blossom. It was a lovely place.

The grass was a variety called *ba-di-cao*, which means 'clinging to the ground', and it was extremely difficult to uproot. My fingers were cut and bleeding from the work. We used spades and hoes but they were useless against the very complicated root system. And even if we did manage to pull it out, after a light drizzle and some sunshine, the grass would make a triumphant return and the ground would be green again.

We had strict orders to remove the grass but the flowerbeds and the flowering trees at the school largely survived. It was in the Cultural Revolution, which started two years later in 1966, that the gardens were mindlessly vandalised and destroyed. Ostensibly, the purpose behind Mao's order was to plant wheat and cotton in place of the grass. And we did plant some cotton in the school. But how much wheat and cotton can a school produce?

Mao wasn't ordering people just to get rid of flowers and grass. China became a cultural wasteland. Opera, theatre, cinema, and books were banned. Across the country books were burnt – in my school too. Mao was much more extreme than Hitler or Stalin in these matters. He deprived us of the classics that Stalin had permitted in Russia and of the kind of apolitical light entertainment that Hitler had allowed in Nazi Germany. Beneath the hot air, what Mao wanted was to create a nation of brutalised, dehumanised, non-thinking, non-feeling slave labourers and denouncers who would attack his enemies.

This happened in the Cultural Revolution. In schools, teachers were beaten, tortured, and imprisoned. Many were beaten to death. In my school, a gardener was beaten to death in the summer of 1966. I didn't see it but I heard about it. He had been an officer in the Nationalist army and afterwards given a job as a gardener, and I believe he was beaten to death by school children because of his past.

By the time I was sixteen, I felt strong enough to reject the propaganda. Although we were completely deprived of information about the outside world, the appalling reality of our lives made me come to the conclusion that the West must be a wonderful place if it was the antithesis of China and allowed flowers and beauty to flourish.

When I came to Britain in 1978 at the age of twenty-six, my first letter home gushingly described the window boxes I had seen on the way from London Airport to the Embassy accommodation in Maida Vale where I was going to live. By then, one could admire flowers in China without being denounced, but the parks were still wastelands. On my first day in London, I took a walk in Hyde Park and the petals of the flowers and the blades of grass made me mad with joy. I was so deliriously happy because for more than ten years of my youth I had lived in a cultural and, in horticultural terms, literal wasteland.

Food

'Anna Maria,' said the old man rat (whose name was Samuel Whiskers), 'Anna Maria, make me a kitten dumpling roly-poly pudding for my dinner.'

'It requires dough and a pat of butter, and a rolling pin,' said Anna Maria, considering Tom Kitten with her head on one side.

'No,' said Samuel Whiskers. 'Make it properly, Anna Maria, with breadcrumbs.'

BEATRIX POTTER, *The Tale of Samuel Whiskers* (1908)

It was a heavenly place for a boy, that farm of my uncle John's. The house was a double log one, with a spacious floor (roofed in) connecting it with the kitchen. In the summer the table was set in the middle of that shady and breezy floor, and the sumptuous meals – well, it makes me cry to think of them. Fried chicken, roast pig; wild and tame turkeys, ducks and geese; venison just killed; squirrels, rabbits, pheasants, partridges, prairie-chickens; biscuits, hot batter cakes, hot buckwheat cakes, hot 'wheat bread,' hot rolls, hot corn pone; fresh corn boiled on the ear, succotash, butter-beans, string beans, tomatoes, peas, Irish potatoes, sweet potatoes; buttermilk, sweet milk, 'clabber'; watermelons, muskmelons, cantaloupes – all fresh from the garden; apple pie, peach pie, pumpkin pie, apple dumplings, peach cobbler – I can't remember the rest.

MARK TWAIN, *Mark Twain's Autobiography* (1925)

I was well aware of the social stigma of our poverty. Even the poorest of children sat down to a home-cooked Sunday dinner. A roast at home meant respectability, a ritual that distinguished one poor class from another. Those who could not sit down to Sunday dinner at home were of the mendicant class, and we were that. Mother would send me to the nearest coffee-shop to buy a sixpenny dinner (meat and two vegetables). The shame of it – especially on Sunday! I would harry her for not preparing something at home, and she would vainly try to explain that cooking at home would cost twice as much.

CHARLES CHAPLIN, *My Autobiography* (1964)

There are thousands of our poor children in London starving, not on account of the poverty of parents, but by reason of the ignorance and sloth of the mothers. They know nothing of cookery, they wish to know nothing. They do not care for the trouble. In every London slum you will find a fried-fish shop, or a cooked-meat shop, or a grocer who sells cheese and pickles and potted things. It is much easier and 'less worriting-like' to send the children out with coppers for a penn'orth of fish and chips, or a bit of cheese and pickles, than to cook anything for them.

R. H. SHERARD, *The Child-Slaves of Britain* (1905)

As a child, my idea of the West was that it was a miasma of poverty and misery, like that of the homeless 'Little Match Girl' in the Hans Christian Andersen story. When I was in the boarding nursery and did not want to finish my food, the teacher would say: 'Think of all the starving children in the capitalist world!'

JUNG CHANG, *Wild Swans* (1991)

I stopped before reaching the garden, and stood sniffing that air soaked with herbs, tomatoes, the clean smell of peas. The garden was a half acre fenced to keep the duiker out, but baboons sometimes got in and threw aubergines and green peppers around, and made holes where they dug up potatoes. The tomatoes sent out a smell so strong it made me giddy. A row of them, yards long, of plants as tall as a man, weighted down with green tomatoes, yellow tomatoes, green tomatoes red-streaked which I sometimes had to pick for chutney – and so many ripe tomatoes there was no hope of ever picking even half of them. I filled the baskets with these dead ripe, heavy, aromatic scarlet tomatoes, added bunches of thyme and parsley from beds crammed full of herbs, and went out, carefully fastening the gate. As I left the birds descended from the trees, and even the sky, where they had been waiting for me to leave, commenting in their various tongues on this interruption of their feasting. Some of the tomatoes had been hollowed out by their beaks, and peapods had opened and bright green peas rolled about the paths. Joan said, 'We don't grow food for ourselves, we are a charitable institution,' and Bob said, 'Birds and animals have to live too.'

I walked slowly back up the long path, feeling the heat get to me, and the tomatoes dragged my arms down. I did not run now as I passed the python's territory, though I watched the grasses for a rippling movement that meant he was coming for me. Slowly I went on, listening to the birds, the birds, the birds of Africa, and particularly the doves, the slow sleepy sound seducing you into daydreams and longing.

I put the baskets side by side on the kitchen table, and drank glass after glass of tepid water from the filter. 'Just make us some soup for lunch,' Joan called from the verandah where she reposed on a long grass chair, another beside her loaded with cats. I filled the grate of the Carron Dover stove, the same as ours – the same as everyone's then – fitting the wood in so there were proper spaces for air, and soon the fire was going. From a hook over the stove I lifted the enormous black iron pot that always smelled of herbs no matter how much it was washed. Into the pot I emptied baskets of tomatoes, twenty pounds or more. The pot was set over the flames, and I went to the back verandah and sat there, legs dangling, watching the wandering fowls, the dogs, if they were there, the cats, whose lives were parallel to the dogs, neither taking notice of the other. Cats had their own chairs, places, bushes, where they waited out the long heat of the day. Dogs flopped about on the verandah, but never in the house, which was Joan's territory and the cats'.

After an hour or so I took the pot off the stove. It was now filled with a gently bubbling red pulp. Stirring it with a wooden spoon in one hand, I fished out bits of skin with a silver spoon in the other. This was a slow pleasurable process. When all the tight rolls of pink skin were out, in went salt, pepper, a handful of thyme and about a quart of yellow cream. This simmered for another hour.

Then, lunch. Platefuls of reddish scented brew, making your head reel with its smell. I did not eat it so much as absorb it, together with the thoughts of the vegetable garden where by now hundreds of birds would be drinking from the water buckets, or fluffing themselves in the dust between the beds. The doves' long slow cooing, the tomato reek, the python – all this became part of the taste.

That's tomato soup. Never accept anything else.

DORIS LESSING, *Under My Skin* (1994)

The Spring Term was always a wretched one, for it brought Lent and, for us, Lent was a depressing reality. We did not fast, of course, but we ate a great deal of boiled cod which tasted no better for being eaten in silence.

ANTONIA WHITE, *The Old School*, ed. Graham Greene (1934)

Growing up in Dublin in the 1950s, I was in love with Marlon Brando. I sent fan letters. I wanted him to come to Ireland, to fall in love with our country and with me. We would, of course, marry and live happily ever after. But I prayed he wouldn't arrive on a Friday, as that was the day our house smelled of fish. You see, in those days, you couldn't possibly eat meat on a Friday or you would burn in hell. We crouched in fear of being somewhere away from home and eating meat on Friday inadvertently. And however badly we cooked meat, I can't tell you what a disaster we made of fish.

Living as we do on a beautiful island whose seas, rivers, and lakes leap with gorgeous fish, did we cook nice fish for ourselves? No, we did not. Fish were meant to be a penance, and they were cooked penitentially.

MAEVE BINCHY, *Guardian* (29 October 2003)

Tapioca pudding is well-known as one of the family of British milk puddings. Like other members of the family, it is sometimes despised by the ignorant, that is to say by persons who have no knowledge of how good they are when properly made. Also, when tapioca is cooked in milk it becomes translucent and jelly-like, causing children to detect a resemblance between it and frog spawn. This may have an additional factor in inspiring distrust.

ALAN DAVIDSON, *The Oxford Companion to Food* (1999)

Tapioca, the grey porridge loathed by schoolchildren, has been remoulded in a heroic role – as a fully biodegradable plastic bag.

Sainsbury's will launch the carrier bag, made from tapioca starch, in April.

Guardian (12 February 2003)

'Hold hard a minute, then!' said the Rat. He looped the painter through a ring in his landing-stage, climbed up into his hole above, and after a short interval reappeared staggering under a fat, wicker luncheon-basket.

'Shove that under your feet,' he observed to the Mole, as he passed it down into the boat. Then he untied the painter and took the sculls again.

'What's inside it?' asked the Mole, wriggling with curiosity.

'There's cold chicken inside it,' replied the Rat briefly; 'coldtonguecoldhamcoldbeefpickledgherkinssaladfrenchrolls cresssandwidgespottedmeatgingerbeerlemonadesodawater − '

'O stop, stop,' cried the Mole in ecstasies: 'This is too much!'

KENNETH GRAHAME, *The Wind in the Willows* (1908)

ALEXANDER THYNN
(THE MARQUESS OF BATH)

When I was seven I was asked by two footmen, 'Tell us, what are you going to be in life? Are you going to be a train driver? A gardener?' 'No, not that,' I said, 'I am going to be the Marquess of Bath.' I could see in their expressions that I had said something wrong. For months afterwards I was working out what I should have said so that when I was next asked – not by them - I had got my answer straight: 'I am going to be a writer who illustrates his own books.'

One of my earliest memories can be pinpointed to my third birthday on 6th May, 1935. My father was driving in Piccadilly and crowds of people were cheering and waving flags. I was standing up in the back of the open car waving a Union Jack and I certainly got the impression that the crowds were responding to me. Only much later did I learn that the other cause for celebration was George V's Silver Jubilee.

There was a special relationship between Queen Mary and my grandfather. As I have been told it, he knew he was going to marry another lady and so he went abroad on a grand tour. When he came back he married the lady intended but Queen Mary and he remained close because of this amorous relationship that did not take off. I can remember going to Buckingham Palace as a little boy and Queen Mary taking me round to choose my present. My cousin Ben had taught me to bow from the waist down but my father said to me afterwards, 'No the right way is just with your head.'

I knew there was a class structure but saw no reason to upset it. It was only later, at Oxford, when I became – not a rabid socialist but much more left wing – that I began to question its basis. At Eton the ambition was to get into Pop where you could wear coloured clothes and tell people what to do. I did all that, so at that time I wasn't thinking it was the wrong model for life; I was thinking more that I was evidently created for success. There was no mingling with anyone who did not come from a particular few schools, the real cream of the public school system. I was awkward with others because I did not know how they regarded me and what my attitude was supposed to be to them. It was class ingrained. It's nothing I teach my children but it was difficult for me to overcome.

During the war, we had a family of evacuees from the East End of London staying at our house at Sturford Mead, near Longleat. They were deliberately cheeky – putting out their tongues – and one was feeling we were losing our pre-eminence in our own house. Feeling their behaviour was unacceptable on our territory, I put a dead rat through the grille that went down by their window in their basement flat. It was done with the idea of gassing them out I suppose. But when I proudly proclaimed what I had done to my mother she said, 'You can't do that', and I was sent down with the head gardener to retrieve the rat. I learnt it was the wrong thing to do. It could have been put in a formal note, I suppose. There was a real divide I hadn't learnt to cross then.

My mother would bring us over to Longleat to lunch with my grandfather. The house was occupied then by the Royal School at Bath and my grandfather had a grandfatherly relationship with all the schoolgirls who were most polite to the person who owned the house. They had been evacuated from Bath and stayed at Longleat throughout the war. There was never any bad feeling – some of them liked Longleat and some didn't – some of them told him it was a horrible, cold house to live in. Their bedrooms are now my spare bedrooms where I have painted the murals of the Kama Sutra. Somebody who had been an evacuee here who remembered the Chinese wallpaper in the room once approached me and complained, 'I'm not sure that I like the way it has been re-decorated!'

I was sitting on a gate eating a banana when Nanny came up and said, 'We are at war'. 'No more bananas,' I thought, 'When will the world get better?' There was an Austrian cook at Sturford who suddenly left for home. She was an admirer of Hitler. Nanny said she used to kiss his photograph which she kept on display in the kitchen. Her name was Miss Schofield and I would like to know what happened to Miss Schofield when she got back home and had the pleasure of being back in Austria. After she left, the housekeeper, Mrs Sims, became the cook. She was an excellent cook. Living on the land meant we were not short of food. We had our own cows – so butter was not a problem – and venison, and rabbits.

I can't remember if it was legal to shoot one of your own rabbits.

It was largely a female environment at Sturford during the war. While my father was away fighting, my mother did introduce the idea of infidelity and there were some males floating through. I remember somebody standing by my mother's bed when I went in to see her in the morning. He was there in his dressing gown. I remember questioning it a bit in my mind – What are you doing in my father's bedroom? I worked it out later when talking with one's school friends about 'what women get up to'. My mummy got up to that, I thought. When my father came back from Africa wounded, he took to having affairs with a vengeance. They both were having affairs, and at the time I supposed that was normal. I was more hit at the end of Eton when my father suddenly announced that he was divorcing my mother, and that I found worrying, surprising. But I felt they had had a try at making a go of it again. I had heard some very fierce arguments and so I accepted that they had chosen to split.

There was quite a lot of bickering between the governess and the nanny. Nanny had been a member of the family and we all had affection for her disregarding some aspects that were a little ridiculous about her. We didn't have affection for the governess, Miss Vigers, but she was far more intelligent than Nanny and one did have a certain respect for the logic that the nanny's children do become the governess's children and that the world belonged to Miss Vigers.

If the children were at the table Miss Vigers or Nanny would have been there too – but not the two of them together. I can remember when Nanny was supposed to send us down to Sunday lunch and I was sniffling or crying at the top of the stairs saying I didn't want to go down and suddenly there was a roar from my father, 'Alexander, you come down here'. All sniffles gone, I went down. From my father's point of view he knew that Nanny was playing a bit of game – 'You can come back to me – just go down – it won't be long' – so he was probably shutting her up. My father would hand round port at table and let me have some from a very young age. I found port delicious. But when my Stanley cousins came to stay my uncle Oliver criticised my father for the waste and afterwards I didn't get port! We don't have it now so it's quite a nostalgic childhood memory.

There were several gamekeepers on the estate. There was a head gamekeeper and something like six others under him. I knew them all but Tom Renyard was the one that my father approached to say, 'Take him out and train him as a blood-thirsty sportsman'. Renyard taught me a love of nature as well as sporting ways – beating for shooting parties, ratting, and rabbiting. I had a Scottie dog called Charlotte. I suppose Renyard's motivation was, 'You have got a dog that never catches rabbits let's see if she can catch it this time'. He broke the leg of the rabbit. I wasn't shocked by what he did but I did ask myself much later why I wasn't more vociferous against it at the time. In some ways, Renyard's pearls of wisdom were wasted on me in that I was not the right pupil. I was interested more in literature and the arts and that wasn't his field.

I did get him prancing over the bracken to catch fritillaries, but he was just joining in because of my interest in collecting butterflies. I never saw a boy with a better collection. I collected butterflies here, and at Eton. They are all called buggers – people who chase bugs. You get used to that word at Eton. I would go out to the woods in Windsor to catch fritillaries that

I couldn't find here. One of my reports said I was taking too much interest in butterfly collecting and so I became sportive. I was intending to be a dry bob, as it was called, but suddenly felt shall we just try being a wet bob? I was good on the river, soon got my colours, and was selected for the second VIII. I boxed for Eton too. I had a straight left, and left hook – the right arm was kept in reserve and seldom used. I had also boxed at my preparatory school, Ludgrove.

At Ludgrove we were all automatically in the Scouts. But it wasn't popular at Eton because it was considered sexually suspect. It was probably tied up with the idea of pretty boys. That subject became a dangerous touchline all round. To what extent am I homosexual? Maybe I am homosexual. Suddenly at Eton I had the feeling that maybe the Scouts would not be good for my reputation.

There were gatherings of the various clans at Longleat at Christmas. There was the meal at the big table and afterwards Grandpa would knock on the table and I had to get up and say, 'All drink to the health of Grandpa!' That was my contribution. These gatherings have not lasted in quite the same form. My generation of Wilsons, or Numburnholmes are now dead, except for Charmian (Bissell), who survived her brothers. So it's now the remaining Stanleys and Thynns.

For a long time I was not the colourful species, so I have tried to catch up a bit. It's the peacock-peahen syndrome, although I do think peahens are beautiful too.

Friends

They were train'd together in their childhoods; and there rooted betwixt them then such an affection which cannot choose but branch now.

WILLIAM SHAKESPEARE, *The Winter's Tale*, I, i., 21–4

It's difficult to convey the full horror of the all-girls party to those who have not experienced it themselves. About half the girls who attended had already decided they were going to be the best dressed, the one who won most prizes and the one who screamed loudest. 'Here comes trouble!' thought my mother as they flounced through the door. Yet this party was by far the least violent of all I had. The girls had not yet got into the full swing of devilry.

Tea was successfully negotiated after a game or two. My mother had prepared quantities of sausages on sticks, tiny crustless sandwiches – ham for the Gentiles, tinned salmon, chicken supreme or fish paste for the Jews. There were tiny fairy cakes covered in hundreds and thousands, coconut bee-hives and individual jellies in cardboard dishes shaped like flowers. They had fruit cocktail set in them and one or two kids turned squeamish at the sight, fearing it might be something worse. My father had prepared jugs of orange and lemon squash, though my mother had insisted on doing the rest. She didn't want black sausages or finger-tested foods.

After tea, Dad pretended to be Charlie Chaplin and somer-saulted over our Egyptian pouffée. Some of the kids laughed hysterically. The humourless ones just glared. Things had gone relatively well till then. Afterwards we played shipwreck in my bedroom. It was never quite the same again. Several girls used the bed as a trampoline to get the wind to huff up their nylon skirts. Others queued in my old white cot until the springs gave with a sad twang. After that it was time to go home and parents started to arrive. Everyone was given a parting present to console the losers – ballpoints, rain hats, coloured combs, etc. By then a few fights had broken out – rivalries over whose nylon was fullest – and a few departed red with rage or full of tears.

FIONA PITT-KETHLEY, *My Schooling* (2000)

. . . I needed lights and the house was exceptionally quiet. Could I hear breathing somewhere? I began to panic. 'This house is haunted.' I still didn't know what that could possibly mean but I felt something unpleasant was beginning to happen. I went on to the landing and peered down the well of the stone staircase, wondering if I could get safely to the basement and the indifferent comfort of the caretaker's. Not a sound anywhere. I tiptoed down the first flight of stairs, holding my breath as much as I could, and waited by the black door of the next flat to see if it moved. Nothing. I took the next flight at greater speed, paused in terror at the second door, and then plunged down the last flight with an uncontrollable clatter and stood panting in the hall where, to my horror, the door to the Ground Floor flat stood ajar.

'Who's that?' asked an old voice, neither male nor female.

I began to back towards the basement stairs.

'Who is that?' the voice demanded, very imperiously.

'Me,' I said. There was a short pause.

'Who is me?'

In my anxiety I forgot my name.

'Me.'

'Come here, Me! Don't be afraid. Me! Come in.'

I edged to the door and gave it a little push which opened it a few more inches.

After some reflection I decided the voice was not unfriendly, and I made my entrance. The room was a large bedsitter, cluttered, untidy and musty smelling; but it was safer than the staircase, more interesting than the basement and had a happier atmosphere than the flat at the top of the building. It was strange, like its occupant, but not sinister.

She was old, shrivelled, big-nosed and very white, and she

lay, propped up by pillows, under a frayed coverlet on a brass bed. Her head was turned towards me, a long, welcoming arm extended and she had an almost twisted smile on her face.

'So you are the little boy at the top of the castle. I hear your footsteps on the stairs. Why do you always run? A young gentleman should *walk*, not run.'

She eased herself a little higher in the bed before continuing. 'Deportment! De-port-ment! Walk with a book on your head, stretch your neck up, up, up; down with your shoulders; keep your b-t-m in, flat. That's what it means, deportment.'

I was more interested in a brass knob on the bedstead, which wobbled as she spoke, than in what she was saying. She was an impoverished Miss Havisham who had lived in a different social world. There was no cobwebbed wedding-cake but under her bed she did have a partially-eaten rice pudding, which she presently asked for.

'Under the bed, Me, you will find my pudding.'

It was in a small, chipped, green, enamel dish, burnt at the edges.

'You've got a lot of fluff under your bed,' I said, handing her the pudding and a bent spoon.

'You must excuse me, Me. I'm an old woman now, dear, and it isn't often I take a broom to things. There was a time – ah! Bright lights! Bouquets! Admirers! Then things were more ship-shape.'

She made an attempt to straighten the spoon. She gave me a confidential look and lowered her voice.

'I had to pop the silver, dear; you know what I mean.'

I returned to the subject of bed-fluff.

'*We've* got a bizzle,' I told her.

'Then you are very lucky. You actually *own* a bizzle?'

'My mummy bought it. In a shop. *We* don't have *any* bed-fluff.'

'Lucky again,' she said, and pushed her pudding aside.

'Do you play games?' she asked. 'Cricket? Football?'

'No, not yet. When I am six. I am nearly six. My new daddy wants me to play games when I am six.'

Her face came closer to mine and her eyes widened in an extraordinary way.

'We are going to be *great friends*, aren't we?'

I nodded.

'You don't find it too dark in here?'

It was fairly dark and I peered round the room; at the standard-lamp with its fringed shade, the shawls draped over chairs, the photographs decorated with artificial flowers, the china objects on the black marble fireplace and the unlit gas-fire. Then I tried to count the wrinkles on her face, but that was a hopeless task and I knew I couldn't count high enough.

'Not *too* dark,' I said, rather bravely.

'It's cosy in the dark,' she said, 'and you can whisper secrets. Will you come and see me again tomorrow? And remember, don't run down the stairs; walk down like a proper gentleman. And when you reach my door knock hard on it and call out in a loud voice, "Overture and beginners, please." Then I shall know it's you. Now, before you go, I'm going to give you a little present.'

She dragged open the drawer of a bedside table, took out a small candle and lit it. The room sprang into life with a hundred jumping shadows.

'That's to light you upstairs. You must leave me now. Goodnight, Me.'

ALEC GUINNESS, *Blessings in Disguise* (1985)

Threes

It was like a dance, a dance of belonging with no private space in it, all inside-out intimacy, and I found it euphoric, intoxicating. And then we would quarrel, for the magic number three is a formula for dissension: two against one, two whispering together, turning away and giggling, the third shamed and outcast. It's obvious now that this was the real point of the whole elaborate dance, its climactic figure, but back then, of course, each quarrel seemed a disaster and I'd run home, tears streaming, and howl on my own back doorstep for hours. My mother, dismayed in the first place by my obsession with such ordinary (if not common) little girls and even more put out by the intensity of my grief when they turned their backs on me, would say, 'It's not the end of the world.' But she unwittingly provided me with exactly the right words. That's what it was, the end of the world, every time.

I cast myself as the odd one out, but in truth it wasn't always so. The real shame that sticks to this memory comes when I recall the pang of pleasure I felt when Valerie and I shut out Jane.

LORNA SAGE, *Bad Blood* (2000)

... I have seen boys in many countries; Egyptian boys in the bazaars of Cairo or mulatto boys in the slums of New York. And I have found that by some primordial law they all tend to three things; to going about in threes; to having no apparent object in going about at all; and, almost invariably speaking, to attacking each other suddenly and equally suddenly desisting from attack.

G. K. CHESTERTON, *Autobiography* (1936)

Playing

We no longer know how to be simple in anything, not even in our dealings with children. Gold or silver bells, coral, elaborate crystals, toys of all kinds and prices – what useless and pernicious furniture! Nothing of all this. No bells, no toys. Little branches with their fruits and flowers, a poppy-head in which the seeds are heard to rattle, a stick of liquorice which he can suck and chew, will amuse him just as much as these gorgeous trinkets and will not have the disadvantage of accustoming him to luxury from the day of his birth.

J. J. ROUSSEAU, *Emile or Treatise on Education* (1824)

Prince of the emerging generation of undersized tabloid favourites is, of course, Brooklyn Beckham, son of footballer David and footballer's wife Posh. Instead of bunging a two-quid packet of luminous stars above the lad's bed, the Poshes added a £20,000 fibre-optic ceiling to a bedroom already painted with 8,000 cartoon characters. As the stars merrily twinkle, projectors built into the wall change the sky's hues from dusk to dawn while the lad snoozes. It was also reported that Brooklyn (who frequently sports Wale Adeyemi and Junior Dolce & Gabbana) and brother Romeo are about to be treated to a treehouse, the £8,000 HideAway Hollow, no less, hand-carved from a Scandinavian redwood and available from Harrods. Well, golly to that.

JOANNA BRISCOE, *Guardian* (18 June 2003)

Thinking over what gave me most pleasure in my childhood I should be inclined to place first and foremost, my hoop. A simple affair, in all conscience, costing – how much? Sixpence? A shilling? Certainly not more.

And what an inestimable boon to parents, nurses, and servants. On fine days, Agatha goes out into the garden with her hoop and is no more trouble to anyone until the hour for a meal arrives – or, more accurately, until hunger makes itself felt.

My hoop was to me in turn a horse, a sea monster, and a railway train. Beating my hoop round the garden paths, I was a knight in armour on a quest, a lady of the court exercising my white palfrey, Clover (of The Kittens) escaping from imprisonment – or, less romantically, I was engine driver, guard, or passenger, on three railways of my own devising . . . I did it for hours.

AGATHA CHRISTIE, *Autobiography* (1977)

Games in the moon. Games of pursuit and capture. Games that the night demanded. Best of all, Fox and Hounds – go where you like, and the whole of the valley to hunt through. Two chosen boys loped away through the trees and were immediately swallowed in shadow. We gave them five minutes, then set off after them. They had churchyard, farmyard, barns, quarries, hilltops and woods to run to. They had all night, and the whole of the moon, and five miles of country to hide in . . .

Padding softly, we ran under the melting stars, through sharp garlic woods, through blue blazed fields, following the scent by the game's one rule, the question and answer cry. Every so often, panting for breath, we paused to check our quarry. Bullet heads lifted, teeth shone in the moon. 'Whistle-or-'OLLER! Or-we-shall-not-FOLLER!' It was a cry on two notes, prolonged. From the other side of the hill, above white fields of mist, the faint fox-cry came back. We were off again then, through the waking night, among sleepless owls and badgers, while our quarry slipped off into another parish and would not be found for hours.

Round about midnight we ran them to earth, exhausted under a haystack. Until then we had chased them through all the world, through jungles, swamps and tundra, across pampas plains and steppes of wheat and plateaux of shooting stars, while hares made love in the silver grasses, and the large hot moon climbed over us, raising tides in my head of night and summer that move there even yet.

LAURIE LEE, *Cider with Rosie* (1959)

Wednesday, 4 January 1871

At 8 p.m. I went out on to the terrace. There was a keen clean frost and the moon was bright in a cloudless sky. Some men were beating holly bushes along the old bridle lane at the top of Parson's Ground. They probably had a clap net and were beating for blackbirds, etc. 'Look out,' cried one man. I could hear their voices quite distinctly across the fields in the silence of the frost. Children's voices seemed to be calling everywhere. I heard them from the village and across the common. A number of children must have been out. Perhaps they were sliding in the moonlight.

REVD. FRANCIS KILVERT, *Kilvert's Diary* (1944)

My Uncle Matthew had four magnificent bloodhounds, with which he used to hunt his children. Two of us would go off with a good start to lay the trail, and Uncle Matthew and the rest would follow the hounds on horseback. It was great fun . . . The child hunt on the first day of this Christmas visit was a great success. Louisa and I were chosen as hares. We ran across country, the beautiful bleak Cotswold uplands, starting soon after breakfast when the sun was still a red globe hardly over the horizon, and the trees were etched in dark blue against a pale blue, mauve and pinkish sky. The sun rose as we stumbled on, longing for our second wind; it shone, and there dawned a beautiful day, more like late autumn in its feeling than Christmas-time.

We managed to check the bloodhounds once by running through a flock of sheep, but Uncle Matthew soon got them on the scent again and, after about two hours of hard running on our part, when we were only half a mile from home, the baying slavering creatures caught up with us, to be rewarded with lumps of meat and many caresses. Uncle Matthew was in a radiantly good temper, he got off his horse and walked home with us, chatting agreeably.

NANCY MITFORD, *The Pursuit of Love* (1945)

LETTERS TO THE EDITOR
of *The Times*

Youthful memories

Sir, I have just spent a wonderful morning with my wife conkering. Though the process gave me considerable pleasure, I was somewhat disturbed by the ease with which we found the usually elusive nut.

Recalling my own grubby-kneed childhood, when one had to thrust deep into the topmost branches with whatever missile came to hand in order to bag even the most meagre of specimens, I can draw only one conclusion. Spotty, noisy, lazy and financially over-developed, today's child can spare no time for anything that cannot be plugged in, listened to, switched on or encouraged to go 'bleep'. Surely the zeal with which I and my contemporaries pickled, boiled, varnished and pampered our most favoured fivers and sixers cannot have totally evaporated in the last 10 years? Can the days of strained trouser pockets and sore knuckles truly be lost for ever?

G. R. E. LOVEGROVE
Nuffield Theatre
University Road
Southampton
Hampshire
October 9, 1989

Conkering heroes

Sir, Mr Lovegrove (October 9) is right. Where are the conker players of today? At the ages of eight, nine and 10 the game of conkers brought sunshine to our lives during the dreary autumn term. There was not a boy in my school who did not play conkers with enthusiasm.

Pickling in vinegar or baking in the oven never produced a great champion. The finest results were obtained only from conkers that had been carefully

stored in a dry place at room-temperature for a whole year. The big round ones were not the best. It was the flat, sharp-edged ones that usually triumphed. The hole must be small and the string soft. The knot must be large, so that it does not get forced into the hole and encourage splitting. A twenty-sevener was the farthest I ever got, and when that one was beaten by a lousy sixer, I was miserable for a week. I can remember a great match that took place on a frosty morning during break in the school yard when a thirty-twoer (Parkins) was playing a thirty-sixer (Arkell). The entire school of 80 boys had formed a circle round the contestants to watch and cheer. When the bell went for the end of break, and the match was not over, the master on duty, Mr Corrado (he ran off with the matron later that term), endeared himself to us all by allowing the contest to go on to the end.

Those were the days.

Yours faithfully,
ROALD DAHL
Gipsy House
Great Missenden
Buckinghamshire
October 12, 1989

JOHN MAJOR

My father had a very odd relationship with radios – or 'wire-lesses' as we called them when I was a boy.

He was a Victorian, born in 1879, and was in his mid-sixties when I was born. By the time I was eight, we lived in two rooms at the top of an old house in Brixton. When it rained the water leaked through the roof, and my father – who distrusted electricity – would switch off the wireless. He would also turn it off if there was thunder and lightning in the vicinity.

The only exception to this resolute response to wet weather was if 'Dick Barton – Special Agent' or 'Journey into Space' happened to be on air at the time. In such cases the weather was held to be benign.

However, it was not held to be benign late one night as I lay in bed listening to an Australian Test Match. My father took the wireless secreted by my side and turned it off – 'Much too dangerous' he told me.

I protested vigorously – the match was at a critical stage. My father – never an unkind man – remained unmoved. I complained. He resisted. I pleaded. He turned me down. I denounced the unfairness of it all and he beamed at my vivid protestations.

Unplugging the wireless, he tucked it under his arm and turned back at the door. 'I know you like cricket,' he said, 'and would like to play for a career. I hope you do – but, if not, you

might consider politics. I think you have the tongue for it.'
And so saying he turned out the light and closed the door.

I have often pictured him in that doorway and reflected on
his words when – in later life – one door closed and another
opened for me.

I remember walking to the cricket ground with our team, sometimes trying to feel, and sometimes trying not to feel, that I was one of them; and the conviction I had, which comes so quickly to a boy, that nothing in the world mattered except that we should win. I remember how class distinctions melted away and how the butler, the footman, the coachman, the gardener and the pantry-boy seemed completely on an equality with us, and I remember having a sixth sense which enabled me to foretell, with some accuracy, how each of them would shape.

All our side were in white flannels. The village team, most of them were already assembled in the pavilion, distressed me by their nondescript appearance; some wore their working clothes, some had already taken their coats off, revealing that they wore braces. How could they have any chance against us? I asked myself . . . And then it crossed my mind that perhaps the village team were like the Boers, who did not have much in the way of equipment by our standards, but could give a good account of themselves, none the less; and I looked at them with a new respect.

L. P. HARTLEY, *The Go-Between* (1953)

THE RT. REVD. DAVID SHEPPARD

In my small study in our retirement house, framed on the wall, is a tiny bib from my earliest years. It has a teddy bear batting – a symbol of my father's hope that I might be a cricketer! I also have a picture that shows the support that came from the other side of the family. My mother was a Shepherd who married a Sheppard – quite confusing. J. A. Shepherd, my grandfather, was an artist who drew regularly for *Punch*, and other journals, between 1890 and 1940. He gave me one of his drawings when I went to boarding school – of the Lions playing cricket against the Kangaroos. It had appeared in *Punch* in March 1895, when there was great interest in the Test series in Australia, with the matches standing at 2-2 – a match that England won!

My father died when I was eight years old, but he had made me a lifelong enthusiast for cricket. He organised a 'Colts' team in the Sussex village, Slinfold, where we had bought a weekend cottage. We played against the 'Veterans Eleven'. Aged eight, and batting number five, I made the top score – twenty-three. I was proud of that. Then the oldest member of the team came on to bowl. Without any warning, he rolled the ball straight along the ground – it was what we boys called a 'sneak' or a 'grubber'. Seeing it coming, I did not know what to do and watched helplessly while it bowled me out. There was anger from members of our team because he had given me no warning, but I had to go out.

I was ten when the war started in 1939. By then, I had watched several of the first-class counties play. But in wartime there was no first-class cricket. In the holidays, I had to entertain myself. Petrol was rationed and most days had to be spent at home. After my father's death, we had moved from London to live in the cottage in Slinfold. I invented various forms of cricket; in good weather there was an endless game against the coal shed door – throwing a tennis ball against the door, and then hitting it as it bounced back. I would imitate the great players I had watched, playing the particular strokes for which each was famous, and wearing my cap at a suitably rakish angle. My mother listened patiently to my account of how each of these coal shed door matches was progressing. In other forms of the game she would bowl underarm to me. My sister was not so cautious. She bowled overarm and rather fast, so that the ball might go in any direction!

I was small until I was sixteen. As a batsman I was beautifully correct, but could not hit the ball very far. My housemaster at Sherborne was a bachelor who was well off. He said that I could drink a glass of his vintage port after lunch each day. When a new housemaster appeared, back from the war, he said he could not afford to give me port, but that I could keep a crate of Guinness in my study. So I drank a glass of Guinness every day. For whatever reason, I grew a foot in the next year! Now I started to hit the ball much harder and had two successful seasons in the First Eleven at school.

After the first of those seasons, an invitation came to play in the first junior county matches to be played after the war in 1945. Young Yorkshire came south and Young Sussex played them in two matches, at Chichester and Hastings. I scored fifty in each game. The Sussex secretary, Billy Griffith, wrote me a letter afterwards, inviting me to come and practise with the county players the following Easter. I carried the letter around in my pocket throughout that winter!

★ ★ ★

I'm a striker; or rather, I am not a goalkeeper, defender or midfield player, and not only can I remember without difficulty some of the goals I scored five or ten or fifteen years ago, I still, privately, take great pleasure in doing so, although I am sure this sort of indulgence will result in my eventual blindness.

NICK HORNBY, *Fever Pitch* (1992)

Training for the end-of-term boxing match was in the charge of 'Mr 'It Me', our sole instructor.

I suppose he was a retired pugilist. Certainly he seemed old, and of an immense size. He had a broken nose, cauliflower ears and the far-away look of a man whose brain had been clumsily manhandled from an early age. He had a huge barrel chest and arms like weight-lifters' thighs. His method of teaching was simple. He would sit sprawled in a wooden armchair wearing a singlet, dirty grey flannel trousers held up by an elastic belt, and boxing gloves. We stood in a queue before him and, as each boy presented himself in turn, he would grunt, "it me!', his only other instruction being "arder!'

We would then step forward and land some puny punch, which must have had all the impact of a butt from a maddened

gnat, on the rock formation of his chest. The majority of these attacks produced no reaction from the dozing pugilist but occasionally, perhaps once in ten times, he would strike back, a huge fist would come out of nowhere and a stunned and dizzy child would be sent flying across the room. These lessons, which were like playing Russian roulette with an earthquake, filled me with terror and disgust. Even if I wasn't struck I didn't relish any sort of contact with the sweat-soaked singlet, and my tentative tap was always met with a deep roar of "'arder!' And rather often, as it seemed to me, the blow would fall, the punch would land, and I would be left with stinging, shameful tears and a headache.

JOHN MORTIMER, *Clinging to the Wreckage* (1982)

I can't help making up things. If I didn't, I don't believe I could live. I'm sure I couldn't live here.

FRANCES HODGSON-BURNETT, *A Little Princess* (1905)

On wet days there was Mathilde. Mathilde was a large American rocking horse which had been given to my sister and brother when they were children in America. It had been brought back to England and now, a battered wreck of its former self, *sans* mane, *sans* paint, *sans* tail, etc., was ensconced in a small greenhouse which adjoined the house on one side ... This small greenhouse, called, I don't know why, K.K. (or possibly Kai Kai?) was bereft of plants and housed instead croquet mallets, hoops, balls, broken garden chairs, old painted iron tables, a decayed tennis net and Mathilde.

Mathilde had a splendid action – much better than that of any English rocking horse I have ever known. She sprang forwards and back, upwards and down, and ridden at full pressure was liable to unseat you. Her springs, which needed oiling, made a terrific groaning, and added to the pleasure and danger. Splendid exercise again. No wonder I was a skinny child.

AGATHA CHRISTIE, *Autobiography* (1977)

I . . . found out very soon that a 'lepist' indulging in his quiet quest was apt to provoke strange reactions in other creatures. How often, when a picnic had been arranged, and I would be self-consciously trying to get my humble implements un-noticed into the tar-smelling charabanc (a tar preparation was used to keep flies away from the horses) or the tea-smelling Opel convertible (benzine forty years ago smelled that way), some cousin or aunt of mine would remark: 'Must you *really* take that net with you? Can't you enjoy yourself like a normal boy?'

VLADIMIR NABOKOV, *Speak, Memory* (1967)

In my youth I formed a deep attachment to the democracy of the waterside. There was the ragged weaver out of work, with his ancient home-made rod, who was out to catch his dinner and kept the smallest fingerlings. He was partial to lures like salmon-roe, and was not above 'sniggling' a fish. But he knew his job, for he knew where trout were to be had, and often he was an expert practitioner in the orthodox parts. But the commonest objects of the waterside were miners from the Lothian and Lanarkshire coalfields. They would come by train on a summer evening to some wayside station on Tweed or Clyde, fish all night and get back to their work in the early morning. Somehow or other they never left with an empty creel. Most were unorthodox in their methods, but not all. I remember one man whose casting with an indifferent rod first taught me what fly-fishing could be. I had many friends among them, and I have shared their supper of bread and cheese, and exchanged a respectable gut cast for one of their strange home-made contraptions, designed for the 'parr-tail', that deadliest of lawless devices. I think pleasantly of my old comrades, who were kind to an inquisitive boy. Like the Black Douglas, they preferred to hear the lark sing rather than to hear the mouse cheep, and there must have been a strong passion for sport and wild nature in their hearts to drive them to spend laborious nights after laborious days.

JOHN BUCHAN, *Memory Hold-the-Door* (1940)

JOSSLYN GORE-BOOTH

I was born in October 1950 at Raby Castle, County Durham, the home of my maternal grandparents. Years later, I found the Visitors' Book for the appropriate period and there was my mother's and father's name on the 4th October and in pencil somebody had added on the 5th October: 'the baby'. I am the last person to have been born at Raby. My mother, curiously enough, was also born there, the first baby to have been born to her family in the castle for hundreds of years. Somebody composed a silly ditty about it saying, 'At last there's a baby at Raby.'

My parents were living in a caravan. This may sound odd, the contrast between the castle at Raby and the caravan being rather wide, but my father was an eccentric man. It has to be said that the announcement of their engagement to be married was not welcomed by my mother's parents. In fact, they did what they could to stop the marriage taking place but my parents did finally get married in the teeth of opposition.

One of the reasons why my grandparents were unhappy about this marriage was that my father had not done very much about getting a job. He took a fourth at Oxford, which is now impossible to do. He had no job, no money, and nowhere to live. This house in Ireland, Lissadell, where he had grown up, was occupied by my father's mother and two of his sisters, and had belonged to his eldest brother, Michael, who by then was a ward of court because he was a lunatic. So there was nothing here for my father. Anyway, he bought a caravan and obliged my mother to live in it. In due course my sister was born at St George's Hospital, on Hyde Park Corner, now an expensive hotel, and after the birth they returned to the caravan which was parked in a lay-by next to London airport – rather an odd place to start your life.

They turned up at Raby in the caravan, my father, my heavily pregnant mother, and my infant sister, the day before my birth. By then things between my parents were clearly far from ideal. My father's behaviour was eccentric, and sometimes violent. I was far too young to know but I remember my mother once saying she got slightly sick of him flinging pans at her head. He and my mother were granted the use of a cottage at Raby in the park and they set up some sort of a home there. There was no money and so life can't have been entirely rosy and, of course, they were under the beady eye of my grandfather who realised that my father was behaving very oddly.

Knowing the family background it was suggested by my grandparents that perhaps my father ought to see a doctor but resolutely he refused so to do. My father's family were not supportive of the idea that he should be examined by a mental doctor. This was regrettable because, as it turned out, he was a schizophrenic like my late uncle Michael.

So divorce proceedings were started by my mother and resisted with quite a passion by my father and his family. In those days, divorce was extremely difficult to enforce against the wishes of the spouse but, after an agonising process, my mother obtained a decree nisi on the grounds of my father's cruelty. One of the conditions of the divorce, set down by the court, was that my father should be denied access to his two children and that my mother was to have sole responsibility for our upbringing, which must have been very painful for him. The divorce became absolute in 1954 when I was four.

I have a picture in my mind of a man in a bowler hat leaning over my cot and I used to think that this was my father. This was my impression but I suspect one's memory plays tricks with one. It was probably the doctor. A lot of men wore bowler hats in those days.

The cottage continued at my mother's disposal but we lived under the roof of the castle: a huge building, substantially medieval. It was originally one of the Neville strongholds but when they took the wrong side in the Wars of the Roses that was the end of the proud family of Neville. Sir Henry Vane the Elder, who was my ancestor and had been a courtier in the service of James I, bought Raby and my mother's family has lived there ever since. The part we occupied after we moved from the cottage was Joan's Tower, after Joan Beaufort, but the main rooms that we used were the Victorian and eighteenth-century rooms.

The original kitchen was almost the oldest part of the castle. It was a vast space going right up to the roof, seventy or eighty feet. It was lit by a lantern at the top and there were some windows lower down twenty or thirty feet above the ground. The only electric light consisted of four thirty-watt bulbs that hung the whole height of the room dangling on bits of old flex. If I touched one, it would swing like a pendulum and took about a minute to go to and fro. The kitchen had an Esse stove but it also had spits, ten to fifteen feet wide, and vast dressers with huge copper jelly moulds and so on. This was where Doris did her cooking. My mother, on the other hand, had a tiny pantry at the other end of the building where she made our breakfast and our tea. Doris cooked our lunch. My sister and I were little children to be seen and not heard, and our lunch took place at half past twelve in the dining room and my grandparents had lunch separately at quarter past one.

Doris also had to cook lunch for a number of people who worked at Raby, including Dale. Dale's job was to sit in the lodge and answer the telephone and then put the calls through to the castle. Dale would walk from the lodge to the kitchen, which would have taken five minutes, and Doris would give him his lunch on a tray, and by the time he got back to the lodge his lunch was stone cold. That was the way meals were conducted.

The local village at Staindrop was a mile away at the bottom of the park. My mother would walk, because she hadn't a car, through the park to the village and go to a splendid shop called Emery & Pratt to buy the groceries to feed us and then once a week they would deliver the stores in a cardboard box, rather in the way modern supermarkets are now doing via the internet.

There were two store rooms at Raby, one had food in it and one had dry goods, and once a week my grandmother would go down and take out supplies for the staff, soap for x, sugar for y, and tea for z, and so on. My mother's stores from Emery & Pratt were placed on a table and, when I grew older, I was always sent to collect them. This meant walking down the bit of the house that we lived in, and down a passage, and through a very beautiful eighteenth-century room with a lovely plastered ceiling called the Stucco Room, and then down a rather nasty stone staircase in the pitch dark to the place where the stores were left. I simply couldn't bear this job. I got the creeps in the Stucco Room and it wasn't until I was older that I realised that I wasn't alone. Many people thought the room was haunted.

Nobody has pinned the apparition down. Going back to the early eighteenth century, the eldest son of the first Lord Barnard made a marriage his mother was violently opposed to. It was the foundation of an important lawsuit, which the son brought against his parents when they started tearing the roof off the castle and burning the furniture because they were unhappy about his marriage. The mother was given the nickname 'Hellcat' and there was some notion that it was the ghost of Hellcat which was still haunting the castle. I never saw anything, and did not experience anything more than a nasty, uncomfortable sensation. Even to this day, when I go there, I feel uneasy.

As my sister and I got older we spent more time with my grandmother and, eventually, with my grandfather. About the time I went to Eton and was wearing long trousers, my grandfather thought I had better come down to dinner during the holidays. His last words to me that I can remember

were, 'One day, young man, I will teach you how to drink port.' He obviously felt it required education and instruction beyond just pulling the plug out and decanting it and pouring it into a glass. He had an extremely good cellar of vintage port. Every evening he would have a glass and, very occasionally, he offered it to other people. If he thought they wouldn't appreciate his port my grandmother would say to the butler, 'You better put out the grocer's port', which was the inferior alternative. I have managed reasonably well without his instruction.

My grandfather was Master of Fox Hounds and my grandmother was also keen on hunting. Whatever your views of hunting, if you're riding to hounds, and the scent is good, and the fox dashes off and the hounds go after it, and you're on the back of a horse that won't stop when it jumps over something in its path, it's one of the most exhilarating sensations in the world. But, having said that, I have no wish to do it again. Most of the time one sat on the back of the horse in the rain and nothing happened at all.

We used to go for a ride on almost every day over the holidays. I took it for granted but I have to say the day in 1966 when I got off a horse for the last time I breathed a huge sigh of relief. We were provided with a series of ponies. They were all rather cheap, and something was wrong with all of them. The first one was called Black Beauty, a beastly little Shetland that was so small it was like a large dog, and it had abominable habits. It used to bite and kick. Another one was called Biscuit (and it certainly took it). And there was a grey which had a disarming habit when you came to a stream of leaning down its head to drink, breaking the girth, and I would go slowly down the horse's withers, neck, and head, and over its ears and into the stream. We used to ride for miles. It was a charming way of seeing the countryside but it put me off buying ponies for our children.

That world is hard to convey because it seemed so normal to me, and still does. Here was this vast establishment with two old people, one middle-aged woman, and two children living in it. But there was also Stannard, the butler, who lived in a cottage in the park. There was Leslie Young, the house carpenter, who lived in another cottage. There were gardeners, even a valet. Years later, I read the *Gormenghast* novels and they immediately brought back life at Raby. There were people working in remote parts of the castle who were operating entirely autonomously but they were all part of this curious world. The staff were extremely friendly and in many ways company for us. We would lark around the place and go and see what Leslie was doing or if Stannard was off duty. I have seen it in similar establishments elsewhere. The staff like continuity and to think the younger generation is coming on.

Most of my Christmas memories are happy ones but there is one that stands out that was not. I must have been in my early teens and, as usual, our younger cousins, of whom there were five, came to tea. After the presents were opened everyone, except my grandfather who didn't take part in these affairs, assembled in the sumptuous but rather formal surroundings of the octagon drawing room decorated in the 1840s in the French style with silk wall hangings and a mixture of Louis Seize and Regency furnishings.

Thinking the evening might be enlivened by charades I suggested we children enact a shop scene and volunteered to act for the shopkeeper. For some reason I felt this required me to open the door of a beautiful, veneered French cabinet and lean on it in a casual attitude. At first this posture seemed satisfactory but not for long. The enormous, exquisite, blue Sèvres bowl, one of a pair, which surmounted the cupboard eased slowly forward and to my horror landed on the Aubusson rug. A meeting of Humpty Dumpty and Marie Antoinette.

After that moment, my memory is much less clear. There were no hysterics but I realised that I had rather dampened the Christmas spirit amongst the grown-ups. The precious pieces of the bowl were collected and later reassembled by Leslie. Nothing was said to me at all but I noticed that my mother looked rather older than she had seemed before. My father-in-law, years later, told me of a similar experience that he had had as a boy playing hide and seek at Chatsworth where he was at a children's tea party. He took refuge in a vast Chinese vase. On this occasion, only the Duchess was witness to the inevitable and she bound him to a pact of secrecy that neither of them would ever tell his parents.

In the build-up to Christmas the carol singers would turn up by appointment. They would appear shortly before Christmas at the big doors and sing a carol outside. Then the doors were opened and the carollers came inside. The hall was a vast, stone, vaulted space where, curiously, we used to have tea. There was a huge table and a fire that was never allowed to go out, kept going summer and winter, day in and day out. The drill was that they would sing a few carols and then mulled wine was produced, and some mince pies. And, afterwards, there were a few more carols and eventually they were ushered out into the dark and the snow.

In a sense, that made a stronger impression than Christmas day itself. Nowadays people push the boat out at Christmas but in those days it was a much more restrained affair. We had Christmas stockings which contained a silver sixpence and a tangerine, nothing enormously expensive. My grandparents were secure at the centre of a vast property but they didn't see themselves as remotely rich, and they didn't behave in an ostentatious way.

I do remember being taken to dancing class with my sister in what was called, with no irony at all, the 'small Rolls'. I suppose there were two Rolls Royces. There was a chauffeur who used to polish the rubber of the tyres with boot polish. By those days, in the mid Fifties, my grandmother had an Austin car of her own. So we were taken to Darlington by her in the Austin or in the 'small Rolls' driven by the chauffeur. We went to an imposing building called the Mechanical Institute which still stands. Somewhere upstairs there was a room where we went once a week wearing silly clothes to be taught dancing.

I suppose it was teaching us to be independent of our mothers. I felt rather ridiculous almost surrounded by little girls.

I always seem to have been surrounded by women. After my grandfather died, I lived with my mother, my grandmother, and my sister, and now I have a wife and two daughters. I can't remember my father's name being mentioned to me but I must have asked questions, and my sister ditto, about him. Many people in those days had fathers who were serving in the army abroad, or in the diplomatic corps, so the absence of a father on a day-to-day basis was not an unusual business.

My father led an unhappy existence. At one point, he was living in a place in Westminster for down-and-outs. Towards the end of my period at Eton, he would occasionally either write to me or attempt to telephone me which in those days was more complicated. My housemaster told me about this in 1966 after there had been a terrible fire in my house causing a huge destruction of property. Being a man of probity, my housemaster felt obliged to tell me that the fire had destroyed letters he had intercepted from my father to me and presents of various sorts.

I raised the matter with my mother and we discussed it amicably. I said I should like to go to Lissadell to meet my father. And she replied, 'Not just yet.' My father went on trying to get in touch with me. At that stage, he was living in a mental home in Banstead, in Surrey, and I can remember one occasion when he telephoned me and spoke at great length and I was too young to know how to put down the receiver.

Naturally I had a curiosity both about him and Lissadell which I had read about and so eventually, in 1967, I persuaded my mother to take my sister and me on holiday to Ireland.

The first time I met my father was quite extraordinary. Not

only was one face to face with somebody who one physically resembled but also it appeared one had inherited turns of phrase, figures of speech, ways of doing things, and gestures. It was like seeing oneself in a distorted looking-glass. Very odd. One realised he was still ill. He took dozens of pills and he was no longer violent but, I have seen this in other people with schizophrenia, he was often very withdrawn.

He used occasionally to send presents to us but they tended to be things that weren't a great deal of use, like a Russian dictionary. And he would write poetry in Russian in his very spidery handwriting but his Russian wasn't very good, and he was a hopeless poet, and so the results were pretty risible.

My great-aunt Eva Gore-Booth was quite a good poet. She also wrote some plays – one was called *The Buried Life of Deirdre*, hardly a title to set the pulse racing. Curiously, there were only two members of my family who were known at all widely. One was my great-aunt Constance, Eva's elder sister. She had this extraordinary empathy with the poor of Dublin. When I was growing up, you couldn't give your name without people prostrating themselves saying you must be a relation of the Countess Markievicz. And the other was my mother's ancestor, Sir Henry Vane the Younger, who was wrongly executed as a regicide in 1662. It's an extraordinary coincidence to my mind that W. B. Yeats, who used to visit Lissadell, wrote a poem in memory of Eva and Constance, and John Milton wrote a sonnet about Sir Henry – 'Vane young in years but in sage counsel old/Than whom a better Senator ne'er held/The helm of Rome'. It's a much better poem to my mind.

I always knew Lissadell would be my inheritance if it still existed but because it was in such a state it was not at all clear it would still belong to the family. As it turns out, Lissadell is now in the process of being sold. We managed to keep it going for rather longer than I originally expected and, in some ways, I am grateful for that. In a curious way, I don't feel at home here.

Many a time I think to seek
One or the other out and speak
Of that old Georgian mansion, mix
Pictures of the mind, recall
That table and the talk of youth,
Two girls in silk kimonos, both
Beautiful, one a gazelle.

W. B. YEATS, from 'In Memory of Eva Gore-Booth and Con Markiewicz', *The Winding Stair* (1933)

MICHAEL PALIN

The family holiday was always a potent experience. I'm not entirely sure what my parents got out of it. A break from the daily rounds and common tasks of a routine existence, the opportunity to recharge emotional batteries that had run low, the simple pleasure of getting up late and having someone else do the cooking and housework.

For me it was always a great excitement, perhaps the greatest excitement of the year, apart from Christmas and the visit of my cousin Hank from Australia. (He was a handsome, dark, dangerous bloke who once produced our cat from inside his coat as he was leaving. We'd never seen it picked up by the scruff of the neck before and my father was furious. Hank died young, in a sports car.)

We were not a family that travelled. There was neither the money nor the opportunity, and seeing the world meant a school trip to Nottingham, or a ride around Sheffield on what was confusingly called the Circular Bus.

Sheffield, where I was born and brought up, is almost as far away as you can get from the sea in England. That's no distance at all, really, but Cleethorpes or Mablethorpe could have been Fiji as far as I was concerned. They say we came out of the sea originally. I must have been one of those who still wanted to get back because I can remember an almost magnetic attraction to sea water and an extraordinary feeling of joy when I first glimpsed it, from Pretty Corner in North Norfolk. It has played an important part in my life, and today, when I remember the battleship grey waves of the North Sea, they're like Proust's madeleine to me, unlocking memories of particular intensity.

I met my wife beside the North Sea, I was walking beside it the night my mother died, I have made films beside it, and written a novel about people who live next to it. Many decisions have seemed a lot easier to take whilst slinging pebbles into it.

So, when did I first see the sea? I reckon it was in 1949, on the first family summer holiday. I was six and because of the war we couldn't afford holidays before that, so it was a double excitement. I went with my father, mother and my sister Angela. Unfortunately, none of them is alive to corroborate all this, so you'll have to take my word for it.

My father was born in Fakenham and chose for our first family holiday the Norfolk coast he knew well from his own boyhood. With children in tow, he avoided the lonely, atmospheric, minimalist pleasures of Blakeney or Cley-next-to-the-Sea and chose the family friendly resort of Sheringham, with its donkey rides and programmes of evangelical beach entertainment.

Sheringham was distinguished by stone-built public toilets of some grandeur, ranged, in splendour, on either side of the steep slope that led down to the promenade. Apart from the North Sea this was the only place anywhere near the beach area to relieve oneself, so my father and I always dropped in and stood side by side at the marble urinals on our way to the sand and sea. He called it 'The Club'.

How did we get there? We had no car (we had to wait until my maternal grandmother died in 1952 before inheriting a fat, friendly, leathery Austin Ascot), so the journey was made by train. Sheffield to Sheringham was not an easy route, even in those days when railways still connected most towns. Our itinerary seemed like the Enigma code, involving changes, as I remember, at Newark, Bourne, King's Lynn, Melton Constable, and possibly Sleaford as well. If this wasn't hazardous enough my father insisted on bringing his bicycle.

Long before PLO meant followers of Yasser Arafat, it meant Passengers Luggage On Arrival and this was my father's preferred method of dealing with the heavy luggage which was sent on ahead (which meant we had to be packed halfway through the week before). This didn't solve all the problems on the day, most of which were compounded by the bicycle. My father had to ride this to the station while we took a large Humber taxi.

At every change on the route he had to race round to the guard's van to make sure the bike was unloaded. It must have been stressful for all of us, otherwise why would a six-year-old remember his father sprinting the length of the station somewhere in the Fens, purple in the face, yelling at the guard as the engine whistle blew?

Beyond Melton Constable my father relaxed. His stammer often made him short-tempered, so on those occasions when he relaxed he was a different man. He loved Norfolk and knew it so well that he could ratchet up the tension as we drew nearer to the sea.

He pointed out how the landscape changed, and the differences from South Yorkshire seemed thrilling at the time. He pointed out the pines and the red-capped walls and the flint-work churches – 'Look, old boy, churches made of pebbles!' Now I can't remember if we were in a train or on a connecting bus but we climbed a hill to Norfolk's highest point (about eight feet), and there through the trees was the North Sea. A blur, a sort of fuzz, and I don't know that I would have known that this was my first glimpse of the sea if he hadn't told me.

I realise that this could have been such a terrible anti-climax, had it not been for my father hamming it up for me. He was a difficult man, and in many ways an unhappy man, but at that moment he was as happy as me.

And those are the moments you remember.

Holidays

Tea was always ready for our arrival, and after the long journey we were always made to get that meal over before doing anything else. Then 'May I get down?' and we were free in paradise, sniffing remembered smells as we ran about making sure that familiar things were still in their places. I used first of all to race down to the lake, to the old stone harbour to which, before the Furness Railway built its branch line to Coniston village, boats used to bring their cargoes of copper-ore from the mines on the Old Man. The harbour was a rough stone-built dock, with an old shed or two, and beside it was a shallow cut, perhaps six feet across and twenty feet long, where the Swainsons' boat, our boat, was pulled up halfway out of the shallow, clear water which always seemed alive with minnows. I had a private rite to perform. Without letting the others know what I was doing, I had to dip my hand in the water, as a greeting to the beloved lake or as proof to myself that I had indeed come home. In later years, even as an old man, I have laughed at myself, resolved not to do it, and every time have done it again. If I were able to go back there today, I should feel some discomfort until after coming to the shore of the lake I had felt its coolness on my fingers.

ARTHUR RANSOME, *The Autobiography of Arthur Ransome* (1976)

Lally was sure that we would get sunstroke while we were shrimping, so we had to wear these awful white cotton 'hates', we called them, which pulled down right over our ears.

'With all this sun burning down on your heads they'll be boiled like a couple of eggs, sure as sure. You wear them until your mother says not. Then it's out of my hands.'

After a day or two we managed to lose them somewhere, but for the first day it was The Rule.

DIRK BOGARDE, *A Postillion Struck by Lightning* (1977)

A part of the infinite charm of those days lies in the fact that we were never bored, and children are bored much more often and much more deeply than their elders suppose.

E. NESBIT, *Long Ago When I Was Young* (1966)

In retrospect, probably nothing that we had as children was quite so important to us as our summer in Cornwall. To go away to the end of England; to have that bay, that sea, and the Mount; Clodgy and Halsetown Bog; Carbis Bay; Lelant; Zennor; Trevail, the Gurnard's Head; to hear the waves breaking that first night behind the yellow blind. I could fill pages remembering one thing after another that made the summer at St Ives the best beginning to a life conceivable. When they took Talland House, my father and mother gave me, at any rate, something I think invaluable. Suppose I had only Surrey or Sussex or the Isle of Wight to think about when I think about my childhood.

VIRGINIA WOOLF, *Moments of Being* (1920)

When we stayed in boarding-houses we didn't actually board but took our own food: screws of tea, packets of sugar and corned beef cushioned by shirts and socks and bathing-costumes, all packed in a bulging cardboard box, cat's-cradled in string and fetched on the train from Leeds. So when we were on holiday there was no romance to the food: we ate exactly what we did at home. Come six o'clock, while the rest of the clientele at The Waverley or The Clarendon or The Claremont would be wiring into 'a little bit of plaice' or the 'bit of something tasty' which the landlady had provided, the Bennett family would be having their usual slice of cold brisket and a tomato. It was home from home.

ALAN BENNETT, *Writing Home* (1994)

Letters to the *Guardian*

Just after the war, when I had no swimming trunks, my mother cut an old pullover just below the armholes, threaded elastic through the hem, sewed up the neck and bingo, a pair of trunks. The idea caught on and the local swimming baths boasted a variety of styles. You had to hold on to your swimwear when diving in or it finished around your ankles.

Peter Evans,
Inkberrow, Worcs

3 September 2002
Peter Evans was lucky (Letters, September 2). In the late 40s my mother (Plymouth Co-op 6873) knitted some swimming trunks from wool unravelled from a pullover. The resulting garment absorbed so much water it had to be held up with both hands at all times. Even worse, a replacement was modelled out of a pair of my sister's school knickers, correctly identified as such by all my male school friends.
John Preston,
Birmingham

5 September 2002
For years I suffered the mortification at feeling I was the only one to have to wear a hand-knitted costume (Letters, September 4). Readers, you have exorcised my embarrassment.
Helen Keating,
Gatehouse of Fleet

6 September 2002
Helen Keating (Letters, September 5) certainly wasn't the only one to wear a knitted swimsuit. We all did. Droopy and itchy. When we cleared out my mother's house I found the pattern. Anyone want to repeat the experience?
Elizabeth Atherton,
Chester

7 September 2002
My mother knitted me a brightly coloured costume when I was 11. After a hot summer's day at the swimming pool, it shrank so much that it fitted the three-year-old girl next door.
Frances Philpott,
London

JEFFREY ARCHER

As a schoolboy, one of my more memorable experiences is of a journey I took during a school holiday, from Weston-super-Mare in Somerset to Leeds in Yorkshire. The purpose of the journey was to spend Christmas with an aunt and uncle who were schoolteachers in Northallerton and, as I had never before travelled beyond Bristol or Bridgewater, I looked forward to the day with much anticipation and relish. My grandmother was one of those early drivers who had not acquired a licence, and had she ever taken the test she would have undoubtedly frightened the examiner out of his wits.

We left Weston-super-Mare in the morning in a large green Morris Oxford. My grandmother drove, my grandfather and mother in the back, while I had the honour of sitting in the front, decades before anyone had thought of seatbelts. My grandmother, like myself, rarely travelled beyond the environs of Weston-super-Mare and for her the roundabout was a new fangled invention which she had not encountered before. We discovered the first one some seven miles outside my hometown, over which she happily drove straight across the middle and carried on in a northerly direction. We encountered twenty-three such obstacles set unnecessarily in our progress, on our route between Weston-super-Mare and Leeds and my grandmother crossed all of them in a manner which would have pleased Hannibal.

On arrival in Leeds, my grandfather who had learnt several

years before not to speak, my mother who was not listened to when she did, and I who did not murmur a word, breathed more than a sigh of relief when we eventually arrived at my uncle's front door in one piece. Once safely on the premises, I ventured the innocent question of my grandmother, 'Surely one should go around roundabouts and not across them?' to which she replied with British certainty 'Certainly not. What you must understand, young man, is that they will never catch on', a degree of logic with which I am quite unable to find fault.

We returned home by train.

Working

I had no stockings and my coat was out at the elbows and hung down to my ankles. I was singing a song by Jean Lenoir:

> *Elle est née comme un moineau,*
> *Elle a vécu comme un moineau,*
> *Elle mourra comme un moineau!*

> (She was born like a sparrow,
> She has lived like a sparrow,
> She will die like a sparrow!)

EDITH PIAF, *The Wheel of Fortune* (1965)

I once saw a child of about seven selling newspapers at Toll Cross on a winter night, without so much as a vest underneath the thin jacket of his coat. He was barefoot. My mother was dismayed. Such children were mostly destined to die of tuberculosis. It was said, I think truly, that their parents drank every penny they could lay their hands on, including their children's gains. Children clustered outside the smelly public houses as we passed, waiting for their elders. I was not exposed to many of these sights but certainly before I went to school I was conscious that others suffered. Poor as we certainly were, there were others greatly poorer, positively in want, and I, in the safety of holding my parents' hands, saw it.

MURIEL SPARK, *Curriculum Vitae* (1992)

When you used to set me off to work in the morning, dressed in my blue smock frock and woollen spatterdashes with my bag of bread and cheese and bottle of small beer on the little crook that old godfather Boxall gave me, little did you imagine that I should one day become so great a man as to have my picture stuck in the window, and to have four whole books published about me in the course of one week.

WILLIAM COBBETT

Where's the little boy that looks after the sheep?
He's under the haycock, fast asleep.
ANON.

We had a little slave boy whom we had hired from someone, there in Hannibal. He was from the Eastern shore of Maryland, and had been brought away from his family and friends, halfway across the American continent, and sold. He was a cheery spirit, innocent and gentle, and the noisiest creature that ever was, perhaps. All day long he was singing, whistling, yelling, whooping, laughing – it was maddening, devastating, unendurable. At last, one day, I lost my temper, and went raging to my mother and said Sandy had been singing for an hour without a single break, and I couldn't stand it, and wouldn't she please shut him up. The tears came into her eyes and her lip trembled, and she said something like this:

'Poor thing, when he sings it shows that he is not remembering, and that comforts me; but when he is still I am afraid he is thinking, and I cannot bear it. He will never see his mother again; if he can sing, I must not hinder it, but be thankful for it. If you were older, you would understand me; then that friendless child's noise would make you glad.'

It was a simple speech and made up of small words, but it went home, and Sandy's noise was not a trouble to me any more . . . I used Sandy once, also; it was in *Tom Sawyer*. I tried to get him to whitewash the fence, but it did not work. I do not remember what name I called him by in the book.

MARK TWAIN, *Mark Twain's Autobiography* (1925)

Tom said:

'Say Jim; I'll fetch the water if you'll whitewash some.'

Jim shook his head, and said:

'Can't Ma'rs Tom. Ole missis, she tole me I got to go an' git dis water an' not stop foolin' 'roun' wid anybody.'

MARK TWAIN, *Tom Sawyer* (1876)

MAURICE SENDAK

I grew up in Brooklyn, New York, the son of Jewish immigrants from Poland. I was the youngest of their three children, an unplanned child. My mother was thirty-one and by strict Eastern European standards, sex after thirty was considered quite unnecessary, if not downright repugnant, but if you must, don't get pregnant and make a fool of yourself. My father told me, 'We tried everything to stop you coming. We bought Momma all kinds of things from the drugstore. And I pushed her off the little stepladder. But you sure as hell were going to come.' Mortality loomed large very early in life.

My father was a natural storyteller and I was put to bed with his wonderfully gruesome stories. It's probably how I inherited my reputation for scaring kids in my books. They were stories of the old world of villagers frightened of Cossacks and of Polish peasants who came with clubs studded with nails. My father never thought for a second that these stories might be inappropriate for his kids. And they weren't!

I was a sickly child, and like most Thirties' children, I was vulnerable to everything. There was no way then to avoid whooping cough, scarlet fever, measles, and all the rest. So I was indoors a lot of the time and my sister and brother would amuse me. My brother Jack wrote stories, and I was hired to illustrate them. Our home was regularly invaded by people called relatives, and Jack would be called upon to read his latest opus and I would hold up the illustrations that I had done on the card inserts for shirts. So I was illustrating stories from an early age. I was his apprentice. I copied everything he drew and I was jealous because I could not draw Mickey Mouse as well as he did. We did spectacular things together. He made breathtakingly complex toys with moveable parts and I would paint them and help assemble them. One was of Little Red Riding Hood, and I have it still. She is standing in front of her grandmother's bed with a basket of food. On the bed is a coverlet, which my sister made, and under the coverlet is the wolf. You pull a lever and the wolf rears out of bed, and Little Red Riding Hood faints. Then you push the lever back up and start all over again.

The big traumatic event in my childhood was the kidnapping of Colonel Lindberg's baby in March 1932. I was four years old, and, as mentioned, sickly. I remember hearing Mrs

Lindberg on the radio pleading with the kidnappers to be gentle because the baby had a cold, to put camphor on his chest, and to cover him with a cloth. I pinned my hopes on the survival of this rich baby. If they found him alive we would be all right, the world would be saved, and I would live. But he died.

The death of the child was a calamitous event. I know children now will be scarred by the towers falling. We are all scarred by some event in history, and mine was the Lindberg kidnapping. When I found out he had died, I lost hope. Here was a rich, gentile child and he couldn't make it. How was I, a poor Jewish child, going to manage? The kidnapping remained in my head and still remains in my head.

My picture book *Outside Over There*, is a replay of the Lindberg case. There is a drawing of the baby in the cave which is a very good likeness of Charlie Lindberg Jnr. But I changed history and the baby is found by my sister and comes home alive. *Outside Over There* is all about my sister being stuck with me, and wishing me dead, but a part of her not hating me that much and wishing me back and so she saves my life. My sister, being nine years older than me, was forced to look after me because I could not go anywhere myself.

When I was eleven, she took me with her then boyfriend to the 1939 New York World's Fair. The Fair was very modern, white and sleek. It just knocked me out. My most vivid memory is standing in front of the Sunshine Biscuit building, a *palais* as I recollect it, and from every orifice of the building the smells of biscuit and cake came pouring out. It was like you had died and gone to heaven. Standing on the balcony of the building there were little people, perhaps they were dwarves, very fat, with moustaches. These Sunshine Biscuit men waved to the crowd and I stood and waved back, waving, waving like an idiot, and when I turned round my sister and her boyfriend were gone. They had dumped me. I went into instant panic, screaming and shrieking, and I was hauled off to a police station where there were many other hysterical children, either abandoned on purpose, or lost. Anyway, I was driven home in a police car and, as we approached the street in Brooklyn where I lived, I asked the policeman to put the siren on for a grand entrance. My mother, meanwhile, had called the whole neighbourhood and told them of my narrow escape. Everyone was on the stoop, the front step, and my mother was hanging out of the window like Cassandra, shrieking and waving her arms. When we got to our house, I was escorted to the door by these three giant policemen and welcomed with hugs and yells. I pointed my finger accusingly at my sister and said she had abandoned me, and she got beat. That is a satisfying memory.

Those little guys on the balcony of the Sunshine Biscuit building are my favourite image from the World's Fair and they appear in my book, *In The Night Kitchen*. That was a goodbye book. When I did it, I was about to leave New York for health reasons. It was a goodbye to the city which I had adored as a child because it was on the other side of the Manhattan Bridge and I could never get there but on the rare occasions when my sister would take me to see some show in the Radio City Music Hall, or to eat non-kosher food in Schrafft's restaurant. It was goodbye to my parents who had died. 'Momma, Poppa,' says the little boy Mickey near the beginning of the book. It was a vision of New York in the Thirties. I put everything in that meant a lot to me. I put in Oliver Hardy. Many people were angry with me for excluding

Stan Laurel but I needed only one fat person. The bakers are there, and so are the little, clumsy aeroplanes my brother and I built as children. It was goodbye to many things. It was also a thank you to the wonderful nurses and doctors who cared for me at the Queen Elizabeth Hospital in Gateshead, England. I had been invited over there for the English publication of *Where the Wild Things Are* and had a heart attack while I was on tour. I was thirty-nine and my then editor at Bodley Head, Judy Taylor, saved my life.

Later, after the book was published and analysed in college papers, those Oliver Hardy bakers with little moustaches were seen as three little Hitlers. Added to the interpretation of it as a Holocaust story is the fact that Mickey is put into an oven and baked. But, unlike the other terrible victims of the Holocaust, Mickey comes out of the oven. He is the hero who finds the right ingredient, the milk for the cake. So he represents youth and salvation for the Jewish nation. Whether this is true or not, I cannot tell you for sure because it was not in my head. I drew Oliver Hardy, not Hitler. But I can see it that way. The Holocaust became the subject of so much of my later work that I have to allow that it was there.

I am the last Sendak. There are no more. Most of my mother's family in Poland managed to get here before World War II but for my father's family it was too late. The whole clan was exterminated. My parents were in constant grief and mourning. My father used to assure me that the Holocaust could happen here. 'Keep a suitcase packed in the closet,' he said. I hated him for taking away the little security I had from living in this country.

It's extremely painful for me to relive these memories in my work but it is a way of giving the illusion that I am in control, and not just a victim. I am like a vulture, I will feed off these memories because that's the only way I can handle them. Something will come, maybe a drawing, maybe a story that will use the memory in a way that is cathartic. It's not for nothing that among my dear friends I have earned the name of Morose Sendak, or Mo for short.

Fear

There were five of us in the family – my father and my mother and my sister and my brother and I – but there were many more people in the house. The red soldiers for instance, who by day were tiny, you could knock them over with a finger, but by night they were ten foot high, came marching straight for you, drumming, and not the least change on their faces. There were people too in the cracks of the ceiling, in the mottling of the marble mantelpieces, in the shadows of the oil-lamps and the folds of the serge curtains.

LOUIS MACNEICE, *The Strings Are False* (1965)

From 'Intimations of Mortality'

The shadows of the banisters march march,
The lovers linger under the arch,
On the beach the waves creep,
The little boy cannot go to sleep.

He is afraid of God and the Devil-
If he shuts his eyes they will draw level,
So he watches the half-open door and waits
For people on the stairs carrying lights.

LOUIS MACNEICE, *The Collected Poems of Louis MacNeice* (1965)

'tis the eye of childhood
That fears a painted devil.

WILLIAM SHAKESPEARE, *Macbeth*, II, ii. 53–4 (1606)

So speaking glorious Hektor held out his arms to his baby, who shrank back to his fair-girdled nurse's bosom screaming, and frightened at the aspect of his own father, terrified as he saw the bronze and the crest of its horse-hair, nodding dreadfully, as he thought, from the peak of the helmet. Then his beloved father laughed out, and his honoured mother, and at once the glorious Hektor lifted from his head the helmet and laid it in all its shining upon the ground.

HOMER, *The Iliad of Homer*, trans. Richmond Lattimore (1951)

All children are afraid of masks. I begin by showing Emile a mask of pleasing appearance, and presently someone puts it on before him. Thereupon I begin to laugh, and, as everybody joins in the laugh, the child laughs as the others do. Gradually I accustom him to masks that are less pleasing, and finally to faces that are hideous. If I have managed my gradation skilfully, far from being frightened at the last mask, he will laugh at it as at the first one. After this I have no fear that he will be frightened at masks.

J. J. ROUSSEAU, *Emile or Treatise on Education* (1824)

Once, on the way there alone, I passed the edge of a huge
ravine a foot deep, where a winged monster as big as myself
attacked me, and I fled and wept. My Father drew for me a
picture of the tragedy with a rhyme beneath:

> There was a small boy in Bombay
> Who once from a hen ran away.
> When they said: 'You're a baby,'
> He replied: 'Well, I may be:
> But I don't like these hens of Bombay.'

This consoled me. I have thought well of hens ever since.

RUDYARD KIPLING, *Something of Myself* (1937)

Gagool

It crept on all fours, but when it reached the place where the king sat, it rose upon its feet, and throwing the furry covering off its face, revealed a most extraordinary and weird countenance. It was (apparently) that of a woman of great age, so shrunken that in size it was no larger than that of a year-old child, and was made up of a collection of deep yellow wrinkles. Set in the wrinkles was a sunken slit, that represented the mouth, beneath which the chin curved outwards to a point. There was no nose to speak of; indeed, the whole countenance might have been taken for that of a sun-dried corpse had it not been for a pair of large black eyes, still full of fire and intelligence, which gleamed and played under the snow-white eyebrows, and the projecting parchment-coloured skull, like jewels in a charnel-house. As for the skull itself, it was perfectly bare, and yellow in hue, while its wrinkled scalp moved and contracted like the hood of a cobra.

H. RIDER HAGGARD, *King Solomon's Mines* (1885)

Gagool I could recognise – didn't she wait for me in dreams every night, in the passage by the linen cupboard, near the nursery door? And she continues to wait, when the mind is sick or tired ...

GRAHAM GREENE, 'The Lost Childhood', *Collected Essays* (1969)

MARGARET ATWOOD

The summer I saw six, we were living in a woodshed on the north shore of Lake Superior. It was a new woodshed, with two rooms and a small iron stove. At that time we moved from forest to forest, and in each location we began in tents and progressed to woodsheds and then to proper houses. We would stay in the woodshed until my father finished building the main house.

We'd been burning out brush on a large bonfire when a violent thunderstorm struck. We ran into the woodshed and waited until it was over. Then my nine-year-old brother went outside to poke the bonfire into life.

Out of the blue sky shot a lightening bolt. It sizzled along the ground, so close to my brother that its wind knocked him down, and struck a dead tree a hundred yards away, shattering it into spears of wood that were driven into the earth. The noise was enormous.

My mother and I rushed out of the woodshed in a state of panic. My brother was lying on the ground. We thought he was dead, but he wasn't. He wasn't even singed, though he seemed stunned, as if he'd been hit on the head. But we could smell the lightning. It was a dry, rasping smell, like burning metal.

Like most undernourished growing boys I was cowardly and I found the last stretch from Clewer to the inn terrifyingly dark and lonely. It was black on the moonless nights and eerie by moonlight and often it was misty from the river. My imagination peopled the dark fields on either hand with crouching and pursuing foes. Chunks of badly trimmed hedge took on formidable shapes. Sometimes I took to my heels and ran. For a week or so that road was haunted by a rumour of an escaped panther – from Lady Florence Dixie's riverside home, the Fisheries. That phantom panther waited for me patiently; it followed me like a noiseless dog, biding its time. And one night on the other side of the hedge a sleeping horse sighed deeply, a gigantic sigh, and almost frightened me out of my wits.

H. G. WELLS, *Experiment in Autobiography* (1934)

The sun had set; an owl began to hoot in the wood. There were many unpleasant things lying about that had much better have been buried; rabbit bones and skulls and chicken's legs and other horrors. It was a shocking place and very dark.

BEATRIX POTTER, *The Tale of Mr Tod* (1912)

To a child who is frightened, the darkness and the silence of its lonely room are only a shade less terrible than the wild horrors of dreamland. One used to lie awake in the silence, listening, listening to the pad-pad of one's heart, straining one's ears to make sure that it was not the pad-pad of something else, something unspeakable creeping towards one out of the horrible dense dark. One used to lie quite, quite still, I remember, listening, listening.

E. NESBIT, *Long Ago When I Was Young* (1966)

Beware the Jabberwock, my son!
The jaws that bite, the claws that catch!
Beware the Jubjub bird, and shun
The frumious Bandersnatch!

LEWIS CARROLL, *Through the Looking-Glass* (1887)

Hush, hush, hush,
Here comes the bogeyman.
Be on your best behaviour,
For he'll catch you if he can.

ANON.

'Hold your noise!' cried a terrible voice, as a man started up from among the graves at the side of the church porch.

'Keep still, you little devil, or I'll cut your throat!'

A fearful man, all in coarse grey, with a great iron on his leg. A man with no hat, and with broken shoes, and with an old rag tied round his head. A man who had been soaked in water and smothered in mud, and lamed by stones, and cut by flints, and stung by nettles, and torn by briers; who limped and shivered, and glared and growled; and whose teeth chattered in his head as he seized me by the chin.

'Oh! Don't cut my throat, sir,' I pleaded in terror. 'Pray don't do it, sir!'

'Tell us your name!' said the man. 'Quick!'

'Pip, sir.'

CHARLES DICKENS, *Great Expectations* (1861)

One Christmas Eve, aged nineteen, Michael Morpurgo sat watching a BBC classic adaptation with his mother and stepfather (whose name he carries), the only father he had ever known since his own father moved away when he was two. It was the opening episode of *Great Expectations*, where Pip slips out at night to meet Magwitch the convict in the cemetery: a scary, atmospheric scene, prisoner in chains appearing from behind the gravestone – and Morpurgo's mother clutched his arm and said: 'Oh my God, Michael, that's your father.'

'It was extraordinary,' says Morpurgo, a tall man wearing his lucky soft-red shirt. 'I've never forgotten it.' His father, still alive, is a Canadian actor. 'It was all rather strange – the first time I see him, he's a convict.'

DINA RABINOVITCH, *Guardian* (28 May 2003)

SYLVIA SYMS

I was one of those thousands of children evacuated out of London by train after war was declared. I was five, and I had no idea what was happening to me. There was a lot of rushing around at the station. My mother was trying not to cry. And then my older brother and sister, and I, were put on a train and sent to some elderly people in Deal. After Dunkirk, we were moved rather rapidly to Monmouthshire, in Wales.

My brother went to live on a farm, and my sister and I were sent to separate homes. In time, the farmer, Mr Phillips, took all of us in, including my mother who by this time was quite poorly, and his family remain friends to this day. My father was a civil servant in the Ministry of Agriculture & Fisheries, and during the war he moved all over the country. So sometimes we lived together with my parents in requisitioned houses, and sometimes not.

Sending me away from home gave me the impression that I was not loved, which is unfair but that's the truth. And ever since, I have always wanted to be loved. It's why I became a performer, and never stopped working. Everyone thinks I must be very rich because I made over forty films in my career but the fact is that women were never paid the equivalent of the men. I was paid thirty pounds a week for making films like *Ice Cold in Alex*.

My mother had a tumour on the brain and, after an air raid on the Woolwich Arsenal Hospital where she worked, her illness developed and she had appalling epileptic fits. The fits were controlled by drugs. Most of the fits happened at night so during the day she didn't seem ill to me, exactly. She was just my mum. But at night, I could be cuddling her in bed and then feel this terrible shaking going on. She always had her marvellous 'mum scent' though – roses, I think, are the closest.

You weren't told things directly in those days. You heard whispers. We knew more about politics and the war than we did about our own lives. It was a very political family. We were different. Other children's parents didn't know people who had come back from the Spanish Civil War with only one leg. We had many more books at home compared with most working class families. My mother used to go to sales of bombed-out houses and come back with a box of books.

She must have taught me to read because I knew how to read by the time I was evacuated. I remember a Welsh school-teacher in Monmouthshire told me I was lying when I read 'A Smuggler's Song' by Rudyard Kipling. She thought I must have learnt it by heart. But my father gave me books of poetry to read from an early age. Mum used to read to us at night because, don't forget, there was no other entertainment. When I was asked to do *Little Dorrit* on the radio recently, I said to my sister, 'It's weird, I turn the page and I know what's going to happen next,' and she told me that it was one of the Dickens novels that mum had read to us. Nobody stopped me from reading any book. I had read all of Aldous Huxley by the time I was twelve and I gave myself terrible nightmares with stories like *Brave New World*. I read also authors like Jack London, and John Steinbeck, never any children's books. Consequently, when I was introduced to children's books at my boarding school, they seemed silly. I could never believe those Arthur Ransome adventure stories about boats.

My mother died when I was twelve. I can truly say I don't know what it was like to be a child. I can't remember ever feeling dependent. It wasn't possible to run home to mummy. I used to envy people who had mothers. So I lived a fantasy life. I wrote stories and plays and performed them. It was a lonely life. There were times on the farm in Wales that were lovely, and my mother was very happy on the farm and fear-less with animals. But I wouldn't want to go back to any day under the age of sixteen.

We have a generation of kids now who, for the most part, don't know what it's like to go without. To me, they are Thatcher's children. You shouldn't blame society on one per-son but many children nowadays think that they have the right to everything and a duty to nothing. That's why it is impressive when these young, so-called, stars do a bit of charity work. They go to somewhere like Africa and they come back with their eyes opened. So many kids don't see anything but their own 'I want'. I have spoilt my own children. If they wanted something, they had it, because I never got the china doll I had wanted. Silly, isn't it, but they had to know they were loved.

My children are the most important thing in my life. Anything wrong was always my fault. When I was having problems in my marriage, I went for some sessions with a hypnotherapist. At one of these sessions, from somewhere way, way, way, back, came a voice into my head, and out of my mouth. It was a child's voice saying, 'I want my mum. I want my mum. I want my mum.' It was as if the separation from my mother, as an evacuee and after her death, before I was fully developed, before I had any security, before I could know her properly other than as someone rather fragile, had never gone away. I have wanted my mum all my life.

First Love

Raspberry, strawberry, gooseberry tart
Tell me the name of your sweetheart.
ANON.

There is a new girl in our class. She sits next to me in Geography. She is all right. Her name is Pandora, but she likes being called 'Box'. Don't ask me why. I might fall in love with her. It's time I fell in love, after all I am 13¾ years old.

SUE TOWNSEND, *The Secret Diary of Adrian Mole Aged 13¾* (1982)

21 July 1931
I have always been in a state of amorousness, unconsciously, since a child, and without sexual consciousness at all until I was nineteen or so. My family still laughs at the story, which I remember well, of when I was five years old, in Berlin, and arranged to run away with a little boy because I had been scolded. They watched me pack my clothes and rolls, and go down the stairs. The little boy, six or seven, was waiting round the corner.

ANAÏS NIN, *The Early Diary of Anaïs Nin* (1994)

Along the shady walks that wound about the cliff gardens of the Spa, at an occasional turn in the path there was a small thatched summerhouse, and in one of these Clara and I used to sit embraced, kissing the afternoon away. At the fireworks on gala nights the rockets would seem more richly jewelled, the golden rain more golden because my fingers would be twined round Clara's fingers. And then there was the pleasure of offering her my four-ounce packet of Rowntree's chocolate creams and my feeling that two hearts beat as one when she agreed with me that the wallflower-flavoured creams were the best; next time instead of buying four ounces of mixed chocolate creams the whole of the four ounces were flavoured with wallflowers.

Commercial television has made the raptures of young love appear more rapturous when offered Rowntree's or Cadbury's or Fry's chocolate creams of today, but I hope the sweets of young love have not become as synthetic as the sweets those lovers munch today. I was talking once about those wallflower creams of long ago to the manager of Fry's in Bristol and he questioned the accuracy of my memory. He had never heard of wallflower as a flavouring. A fortnight later I received a charming letter from him to say I had been right and that he had found an almost empty bottle of the essential oil of wallflowers with just enough for a couple of pounds of chocolate cream which he was sending me in the hope that it might bring back a flavour of once upon a time.

COMPTON MACKENZIE, *My Life and Times* (1963)

Private Parts

There was a slab outside the dining room door for standing dishes upon. Once when I was very small Gerald Duckworth lifted me on to this, and as I sat there he began to explore my body. I can remember the feel of his hand going under my clothes; going firmly and steadily lower and lower. I remember how I hoped that he would stop; how I stiffened and wriggled as his hand approached my private parts. But it did not stop. His hand explored my private parts too. I remember resenting, disliking it – what is the word for so dumb and mixed a feeling? It must have been strong, since I recall it. This seems to show that a feeling about certain parts of the body; how they must not be touched; how it is wrong to allow them to be touched; must be instinctive.

VIRGINIA WOOLF, *Moments of Being* (1920)

Then there was the pain. A breaking and entering when even the senses are torn apart. The act of rape on an eight-year-old body is a matter of the needle giving because the camel can't. The child gives, because the body can, and the mind of the violator cannot.

MAYA ANGELOU, *I Know Why the Caged Bird Sings* (1969)

Mr Dodd was almost entirely beige. A beige raincoat, beige face, beige hair and freckles. He sat two or three seats away from me and smiled pleasantly all through the Forthcoming Attractions. And I still didn't know.

During the interval, when the lights went pink and green and the organ rumbled through a selection from something or other, he smiled shyly across the empty seats and I smiled back, and he moved along and came and sat beside me. He asked if I would like an ice-cream, and I said yes, and we ate together in pleasant, companionable silence. He was very polite, quiet spoken and smiled a lot; and when he took my empty ice-cream tub away from me, plus the wooden spoon and stacked it neatly into his own and tidily placed it all under his seat, he patted my leg kindly and whispered with a secret wink that I was, in all probability, playing truant from school, wasn't I? Shattered with surprise that he so quickly found me out, I lied swiftly and said that I was 'off school' with a sprained ankle. That seemed to content him and the programme started again so that there was no need for more conversation.

It was very nice having someone to laugh at the film with, to share fear with, and to enjoy relief with all at the same time. He was very attentive and once, in a particularly creepy part he put his arm protectively round my shoulder, which I felt was very thoughtful of him indeed.

DIRK BOGARDE, *A Postillion Struck by Lightning* (1977)

In the village Mr Bowles fulfilled the perfect image of the squire, doing good works, holding the church as well as he could together, but above all interesting himself in the religious education of the boys for whom he conducted weekly confirmation classes in his house.

Every boy in the village, without exception and including myself, attended these classes, purely because of the irresistible benefits they entailed, although I cannot remember a single one who after confirmation bothered any more with the church. A series of ten classes were held and, as we saw it, it was worth putting up with the boredom of nine of them for the top-rate entertainment offered by the tenth, on the subject of sex. In this class Mr Bowles discussed the facts of life with extreme frankness, and we had learned from boys attending the classes of previous years of an interesting demonstration he could be encouraged to give if faced by what he believed to be total incomprehension. For this purpose he kept ready two antique French dolls, and when at our last class there were cries from us of, 'He doesn't understand, sir. Show him your jig-a-jig,' Mr Bowles unlocked and opened a drawer under his birds' egg cabinet and took these out. In the rather solemn and awestruck tone he normally used for reading the lesson in church, he drew our attention to the manner in which they were joined together. After that, a match was put to the combustion chamber of a tiny steam engine fuelled by cotton wool soaked in methylated spirits, to which the dolls were connected, and soon the tiny hips started to bounce, first slowly, then frantically as the engine warmed up, till finally with an ecstatic squeak of steam through a valve it was all over. A brief prayer in which we all joined followed, and our preparation for life was at an end.

NORMAN LEWIS, *I Came I Saw* (1985)

What a Boy Should Know

A boy who practices this habit can never be the best that Nature intended him to be. His wits are not so sharp. His memory is not so good. His power of fixing his attention on whatever he is doing is lessened. His mind will wander from his work or go 'wool-gathering,' as it is called. His decision, or the power of making up his mind, is diminished, and his self-confidence and reliance leave him. Instead of being alert, quick-witted, and attentive, his mind becomes slow and slack. His thoughts are undetermined and have no grip. A boy like this is a poor thing to look at.

If his condition is the result of ignorance he is to be pitied. If his condition is not due to ignorance, but simply because he has become the victim of a habit, he is still to be pitied if he fails to overcome it. But if he wilfully persists in doing what he knows is harmful just for the sake of the pleasure it gives him – well, he deserves all he gets. He will probably be bottom of his class and get many a licking. He will surely be a duffer at games and it is a hundred to one he gets laughed at more than any boy in the school for his blundering stupidity.

ALFRED TAYLOR SCHOFIELD and PERCY VAUGHAN-JACKSON, *What a Boy Should Know* (1913)

Compiler's note: Dr Schofield also gave lectures to Scout-masters as an aid to training in the early days of the Boy Scout Movement.

Schoolmaster: Well, Foster, here at St Onan's I usually try to make my last Confirmation Class rather more of a personal chat than a theological thing. Now Foster . . . look, we've been through the 39 Articles together, we know each other pretty well, I don't want to go on calling you Foster. What's your nickname? What do your friends call you?

Foster: Nitbags, sir.

Schoolmaster: Well, Foster, what I want to tackle now is this problem of your body. Now your body is laid out on fairly simple straightforward lines, isn't it? You've got your two arms, and your two legs, here's that valiant worker the heart and his two stout cronies the lungs. It's all pretty straightforward.

Foster: Yes, sir.

Schoolmaster: And here we come to the crux. You're not embarrassed about this are you, Foster? There's no need to be embarrassed about it. You're a bright observant sort of lad, you've probably noticed when you've been slipping into your togs or getting into your little jim-jams, that when you get down here things aren't straightforward at all?

Foster: Yes, sir.

Schoolmaster: Good, good. And I suppose you must have wondered how it is that God, who by and large made such a splendid job of the rest of your little body, made such a bosh shot at that particular bit?

Foster: Yes, sir.

Schoolmaster: Well, I agree with you. But God, whatever else He is, and of course He is everything else, is not a fool. It's not pretty, but it was put there for a purpose. Point taken, Foster?

Foster: Yes, sir.

Schoolmaster: Good, well I think that clears up any doubts

you might have had on that particular subject. Just one
moment, Foster. I know you're a bit of a scallywag . . . anything
I say to you will probably just go up one trouser leg and down
the other. But remember this. That particular piece of appara-
tus we've been exploring is called your private parts. And
they're called that for a reason. It's not that they're anything to
be ashamed of. They're not . . . though they're not anything to
be proud of either. They are private because they are yours and
yours alone.

(*He moves his chair nearer the boy's.*)

And you should keep them to yourself.

(*And nearer still.*)

If anyone else touches you there that person is wicked.

(*He places his hand on Foster's knee.*)

No matter who it is, you should say to him that belongs to
me. It is my property. You have no business to touch it.

Foster: That belongs to me and you have no business to
touch it.

Schoolmaster: Doesn't apply to me, Foster. (*Hitting him.*)
Doesn't apply to me.

ALAN BENNETT, *Forty Years On* (1969)

Thirty-Four Years On

The Commons health committee yesterday took evidence from
a dozen teenagers, whom they asked about sex education, sex
problems, sex advice and, while they were on the subject, sex.

It's the kind of occasion that can be a toe-curling, buttock-
clenching, bowel-loosening embarrassment, which of course
is why I went along.

As I arrived an earnest young man was demanding gay sex education from gay sex teachers. The young persons had other requests, including full-time sex educators, text messaging services ('If I can get texts on how my football team is doing, why not sex advice?') plus free condoms and bus fares to sex clinics.

The MPs nodded earnestly at all this and smiled the glassy smiles of Old Persons in the presence of Young Persons, who can be allowed to say anything they like and still receive encouraging nods.

Some of the Young Persons belonged to the National Youth Parliament, which is full of the kind of people who, in 20 years or so, will be in the real parliament, asking similar questions to Young Persons yet unborn. They have all the patter, about 'peer research', 'receiving input', and 'summarising key positions'.

Yet in spite of this there was a tremendous gulf between the legislators and some of these eager Young Persons. Simon Burns, one of the two Tories on the committee, was told that some schools won't let girls who have just had sex out of lessons in order to buy the morning after pill.

'Can't they tell their parents, over breakfast?' he asked. As a shout of laughter came up from MPs and Young Persons alike, I yearned for him to add: 'or at least have a word with the butler'.

And then there was Sarah. Sarah is 18, and comes from Wakefield. She is a big lass with a confident, even forceful manner, and an ability to dominate everyone within 100 yards.

Sarah is a type I know well from my northern childhood, a woman who takes no nonsense from men, who quail before her tread. Ena Sharples was the template, but they still churn them out as fast as they once produced rolls of worsted in

Wakefield. She could devour a bunch of nervous MPs as easily as she would down a bag of chips.

Sarah hardly stopped talking. The other Young Persons fell silent as she described her contempt for all forms of sex instruction. 'I remember because when I was 13 on the street with my bottle of cider, and phoning, and it said "Sex Line!" and I said "Ha, ha, sex line!" and rang off.'

As for using the internet, 'they can't access that at school because sex is bad and you can't get anything if it says "sex", unless they're using it at home, and I know my Dad can access everything I do on the internet, and willingly reads my emails'.

Mr Burns tried again.

'When you talk about sex, do you mean "snogging" or, er, sexual intercourse?'

Sarah flipped him aside.

'Snogging's not a big thing any more. It used to be if you went out and you snogged a bloke it would be, like "Yes! I snogged a bloke!" but now you snog a bloke and then it's "I've snogged another bloke" and, "yes, I've slept with a bloke".'

She warmed up. 'I knew a bloke; he'd slept with 50 people, and the 50th was on his 17th birthday. Well, it's not big and it's not hard.'

The temptation to say, 'but surely it must be?' was immense and resisted.

SIMON HOGGART, *Guardian* (17 January 2003)

Philip and Martin came in, their expressions quite blank, innocent in every possible way that the most expensive film-director could have put there. They were, I suppose, seven and six years old. The short monologue I gave them slipped out of my head afterwards at the first opportunity, though I know I did conscientiously get in a certain amount of what might be called hard anatomy and concrete nouns, although again I must have used the word 'thing' a good deal and talked about Dad planting a seed. Well, what would you? I have never loved and admired them more than for the unruffled calm and seriousness with which they heard me out. I knew they knew, they knew I knew they knew and so on to the end but never mind. They left in a silence that they courteously prolonged until they were out of all hearing. It was a couple of years before Philip confided to me that he had muttered, 'Hold on to your hat – he's going to tell us the big one' as the two made their way to my 'study'. But we did it. In no sphere is it truer that it is necessary to say what it is unnecessary to say.

KINGSLEY AMIS, *Memoirs* (1991)

I am not having you on. My parents still have my foreskin in a plastic container.

MARILYN MANSON, 'Friday Night With Jonathan Ross', BBC1 (6 June 2003)

Violet Lane was a chorus girl dancer in the flicks of the Thirties, pin-curled, shining, resplendent and just, just five foot tall. Most of her was legs, yet she also possessed an impressive bosom that looked as if it had been placed upon her as the almost implausible afterthought of her creator, so tiny was she. Her laugh though, was big and delighted (as if she had discovered an amusing secret), her angers were few and disguised. She was 'Laney' to her friends, 'Mrs Holloway' when she married, 'mummy' to my father (her only child) and 'Gee-Gee' to me. The origins of this name are mysterious, rooted probably in that tender tongue of babyhood. She was never 'Violet'. She loathed the name with passion all her life.

Gee-Gee lived in an oversized doll's house that watched the sea in West Sussex. From her bedroom you could look over the high garden wall through the trees that sang and whispered wild sea-songs and see the grey waves that danced up to the shingle then ran away. The rooms of her house contained mysteries and things within things; stools that opened, a stone that was pink when it was fair weather and moody blue when a storm was coming. Silver boxes filled incongruously with Cadbury's chocolate eclairs and lemon sherbets. More silver boxes filled with cigarettes.

The dressing room was made for hide-and-seek, with trap doors and small places and big fur coats that you could hide under, their pockets always filled with crumpled tissues and pennies. The sitting room had a curious smell the morning after the night before, of whisky and cigars, an adult smell that made Gee-Gee say 'POOH' and throw open the windows dramatically when we came down for breakfast on Sunday mornings. I wondered wordlessly where they had come from, these cigarette-wielding grown-ups who left the bones of their party behind. Did they come in the middle of the night while I slept, tiptoeing off moments before I opened my eyes?

'Going to Gee-Gee's' happened every other weekend that I spent with my dad. With the unbridled narcissism that stems from being six and an only child, I couldn't imagine how Gee-Gee spent her days and survived during the times we were not there. I wrote her postcards from London and worried about it.

The best thing about going to Gee-Gee's was Sunday mornings. Sunday mornings were glorious. I would wake and charge up the stairs in my nightie like a sturdy gymkhana pony, but clumsy with glasses. Bursting through the door I would throw myself with great fervour on the tiny form buried under swathes of blankets that was Gee-Gee's bed. The Gee-Gee bed was filled with an arsenal of warming devices as she suffered from terrible circulation and a perilous fear of the cold. Her bed was not really a bed, but more of a nest. In the nest were:

  two hot water bottles
  one sheet
  two blankets
  three eiderdowns

and Gee-Gee clad in thermal long-johns. (In the summer

the nest remained the same minus one hot water bottle – the thermals exchanged for a silk peignoir.)

Out of all of this she would flutter, opening one eye, wiggling her feet. 'Good morning, darling. Is it time for *Rub-a-dub-dub?*' which was a programme I adored. We would lie with a tea tray between us, my warm feet entwined with hers, which like the rest of her were of course small but perfectly formed and, despite hot-water bottles, cold. And it was in those moments of love, with the pale winter sun shining into her apricot-coloured bedroom, snuggled against her soft body that I learned what it was to feel perfect, blissful contentment, as the sea swelled a lullaby that carried me through childhood.

Grown-ups

I had a vindictive dislike of grown-up persons, however kindly, who tried to be witty at my expense (by asking, for example, 'Who was the father of Zebedee's children?').

ARTHUR RANSOME, *The Autobiography of Arthur Ransome* (1976)

New Year's Day 1946
My children weary me. I can only see them as defective adults; feckless, destructive, frivolous, sensual, humourless.

EVELYN WAUGH, *The Diaries of Evelyn Waugh* (1976)

Some children can remember their fathers reciting Urdu poetry or Marlowe, or teaching them to recognise birds and butterflies, to spot trains, to play chess or cricket. But you, Daddy dear? Not a curve-ball, not a cover-drive, not a card-trick. Not a maxim. Not a saw, adage or proverb. Except, 'You're big enough and ugly enough to take care of yourself.' This is my *Enchiridion Militis*, my soldier's breastplate.

GERMAINE GREER, *Daddy, We Hardly Knew You* (1989)

We kept Mommy on a pedestal – it was the only way we could keep Daddy from her.

DOLLY PARTON, *Observer* (24 November 2002)

When does the sad decline into dadishness begin? For me, it started three years ago, when my son Laurence (two years older than his sister) made the transfer to secondary school. 'There is no need to come to the school gate,' he told me on his mobile, as I set off to collect him one afternoon. 'You know that road next to the car park? Wait for me there.' We had always been a tactile family, exchanging physical affection easily, so this sudden self-consciousness was unnerving. Resisting the urge to embrace, or even ruffle Laurence's hair, I stood awkwardly with arms akimbo and suggested we get a bus home rather than walk. 'No we can't – that's the bus my friends get.'

Was I really so mortifying to be seen with? In my mind, I was a youthful, reasonably hip parent, in my Firetrap jacket, Timberland boots and designer stubble – far less embarrassing than all those portly M&S-suited dads with shiny heads and florid complexions, lined up in their Volvo estates. I must have looked ten years younger than that lot.

'Why don't you want to be seen with me?' I asked. 'It's not the way you look, Dad,' Laurence told me. 'It's just that you kind of sing all the time.'

The thing that really bugged me, though, was that they never wanted to go anywhere . . . Only during a rare encounter with another father of teenagers did I fully understand the dynamics of sloth. 'It's not that they don't want to do anything,' he explained, 'it's just that they don't want to do it *with you.*' Only my children could have put it more witheringly. To them I was a bouncy castle has-been, a pointless social embarrassment, someone who danced badly at parties and listened to outdated music.

ANDREW PURVIS, *Guardian* (12 February 2003)

School was my world, and I can only remember a single occasion on which my parents intruded – this was when my father decided he wanted to watch the school's football team play Charterhouse. He had seen, in *The Times*, an article about the centenary of this fixture.

'Parents never watch matches,' I explained, 'and the boys only watch because they're told to. Sport isn't highly regarded at Westminster.'

'Why is that?' My father looked confused.

'Because boys who like games are usually dull.'

'I loved football as a boy.'

'I'm really sorry, daddy. I'm sure some of the first team are nice. But you really mustn't come. It's too difficult to explain, and you wouldn't understand it if I tried.'

On the day of the match, I'd almost forgotten our conversation – in fact, I'd become quite involved with the football. But in the second half, the game became scrappy and my attention wandered. There was a children's hospital in Vincent Square, beside our playing field, and I spotted several sick boys gazing down at the game. To the left of the hospital, a man was standing on the steps of an ordinary house. I thought he was my father's double, but only for a moment.

A better boy than I was would have brought his father in through the gates at once – even *I* had to struggle hard not to do the decent thing. But somehow I managed to avoid looking in his direction until the game was over. Even now, I sometimes wish I had risked the ridicule of my peers.

TIM JEAL, *Swimming with My Father* (2004)

It was indeed the beginning of a mild persecution – very mild and concealed in smiles and kindly faces; the grown-ups could not have known it was one. But it became the thing to say to me, when they came across me, 'Hullo, Leo, still feeling hot?' And 'Why don't you take your jacket off – you'd be more comfortable without it' – with a light laugh for this impossible request, for in those days dress was much more ceremonious and jackets were not lightly discarded. I came to dread these pleasantries, they seemed to spring up all round me like rows of gas-jets scorching me, and I turned redder than I was already. The frightful feeling of being marked out for ridicule came back in all its strength. I don't think I was unduly sensitive; in my experience most people mind being laughed at more than anything else. What causes wars, what makes them drag on so interminably, but the fear of losing face?

L. P. HARTLEY, *The Go-Between* (1953)

Questions . . .

Like all Xhosa children, I acquired knowledge mainly through observation. We were meant to learn through imitation and emulation, not through questions. When I first visited the homes of whites, I was often dumbfounded by the number and nature of questions that children asked their parents – and their parents' unfailing willingness to answer them. In my household, questions were considered a nuisance; adults imparted such information as they considered necessary.

NELSON MANDELA, *Long Walk to Freedom* (1994)

And answers . . .

This is from *I Like It Here* (1958), Kingsley's third and most close-to-life novel.

'Dad.'

'Yes?'

'How big's the boat that's taking us to Portugal?'

'I don't know really. Pretty big, I should think.'

'As big as a killer whale?'

'What? Oh yes, easily.'

'As big as a blue whale?'

'Yes, of course, as big as any kind of whale.'

'Bigger?'

'Yes, much bigger.'

'How much bigger?'

'Never you mind how much bigger. Just bigger is all I can tell you.'

There is a break, and the discussion resumes.

. . . 'Dad.'

'Yes?'

'If two tigers jumped on a blue whale, could they kill it?'

. . . 'Oh, God. Well, I suppose the tigers'd kill the whale eventually, but it'd take a long time.'

'How long would it take one tiger?'

'Even longer. Now I'm not answering any more questions about whales or tigers.'

'Dad.'

'Oh, what is it now, David?'
'If two sea-serpents . . .'

MARTIN AMIS, *Experience* (2000)

Letters to the Guardian

9 December 2003

More than 70 years ago, my dad asked me to punctuate 'that
that is is that that is not is not that that is is not that that is not
that that is not is not that that is that is it is it not'. Quite a
challenge to ask a 10-year-old. I can't remember whether I got
the answer right, although I suspect I didn't.
Gerry Cohen
London

10 December 2003

Can someone please punctuate, correctly if possible, Gerry
Cohen's sentence (Letters, December 9). I was lost before the
fourth 'is'.
Dave Harris
Potters Bar, Herts

11 December 2003

That that is is; that that is not is not; that that is is not that that
is not; that that is not is not that that is; that is it, is it not? Less
than 5 seconds.
Shirin Patel
Bombay

MARINA MAHLER

As a child living in London, I heard a lot of music. In the home, my mother played the piano, as did my father, we listened to the radio, and we went regularly to rehearsals and concerts. Music was an integral part of our lives.

My father was the conductor, Anatole Fistoulari. He was eccentric and very gentle, and I still come across musicians who remember him with pleasure. When I go back after a Mahler or some other concert, they say to me, 'Oh, you are Fisti's daughter,' and they tell me a story about him. His family were White Russians and they had to leave Kiev under duress, when my father was about twelve, to escape the revolution.

My name, Marina, my father took from the opera *Boris Godonov*, after the dreadful Polish princess, and my second name, Elisabeta, he chose after Queen Elizabeth! That was my father's desire, and my mother agreed to it. He loved all Russian opera. The first opera I heard, when I was three years old, was a rehearsal of Tchaikovsky's *Eugene Onegin*, and it remains one of my favourites. I was allowed to attend his rehearsals, and one of my first memories is of standing next to the conductor's podium and wandering about under the musicians' stands on the stage.

When I was seven I left England, much to my deep sadness. I travelled by boat with my mother to New York, and from there by train to California. My mother told me it was just a visit, but I knew it was more than that, and my reaction was to refuse food. Children know much more than you imagine. I didn't see my father again until I was eighteen when my mother sent me to England to meet him.

America was a big shock. We had gone there to live with my now very famous grandmother, Alma Mahler, who lived in Beverley Hills, next door to the conductor, Bruno Walter, who had a swimming pool and comforted me with jam tarts and other sweets. Alma was neither a very good grandmother, nor had she been a good mother. But I didn't notice because she was so beautiful. She was luminous. I was asked to call her 'mother' because she did not want to be known as a grandparent. So I had acquired suddenly two mothers.

I went to Ojai Valley School, a co-educational boarding school up in the mountains near Santa Barbara where we led an active outdoor life. There were horses, tennis courts, a swimming pool, trees to climb in the extensive grounds, and a farmyard where it was my job to care for some ducks. The landscape was wonderful. Every year the children went on a ten-day camping trip. We used to put our packs on our backs and walk for miles into the hills, and then pitch our tents. We washed our hair and swam in the pure, clean, cold water of the Sespe river. In the evening, we roasted marshmallows and chocolate on sticks over the open fire and when they were melting put them on graham crackers. This lovely sweet was called 'riders on horseback' for some odd reason. We watched the bats descend, and told ghost stories in the dark. In the morning, we pulled ticks out of our tummies using a lighted match to coax them out backwards. I was happy.

When my grandmother moved to New York, my mother and I went to live up in the hills in the rather wild, no man's land, north of Sunset Blvd. My mother would rise very early to work on her sculpture in the outdoor parking lot which served as a stone carving studio, and then she would come in later and eat her second breakfast with me. If she was busy, I would go to my room to read or write, which I loved to do. It was the perfect existence because I had such a lot of silence for myself. Often I helped her by sweeping up the fallen chips into boxes while she was chipping away with hammer and chisel. Nothing could have been more beautiful because I had the life next to her. She did her work, and that left me free. Nothing was asked of me. I had the most wonderfully private dreaming time, when I wasn't at school.

There are always difficult times to deal with in childhood but I don't think sadness is in itself wounding. Sadness makes us think, and reflect, and develop. But I do think ugliness and cruelty are wounding and harder to overcome in later life. Sadness, separation, loneliness, even death, these kinds of unhappiness you can deal with. I didn't blame my mother for this sadness. She had to follow her life, to leave my father, and to go to her mother, and I was the child she took with her into this new life, and new world. She suffered too. I remember seeing her cry.

I missed England, and my life there, very much all the time I was growing up in America. Every once in a while my father used to send me the most extraordinary squashed package covered in stamps. Sometimes it had the most amazing chocolates inside, as squashed as the package, but the fragrance was overwhelming. Once I got an Easter egg. The packages used to come, not every year, but occasionally - signed 'Love, Daddy' - and their rarity made them even more special. I still adore getting packages in the post. The things that excited you as a child, you take with you into adult life.

I did blame him, of course. Why wasn't he there? Why didn't he come and see me? But at the same time I accepted his absence. I invented a father of whom I was very proud. At some point, I used to tell people he was a pilot in the Air Force. I don't know why I said this. Of course, he had never flown a plane in his life.

The life my mother and I led in California had nothing to do with the past. There were no photographs in our home. My mother was trying to escape from the huge shadow of her father, Gustav Mahler, and from her difficult mother, Alma Mahler Werfel, who demanded adoration which my mother was loath to give. For me, the greatness of Mahler, the responsibility connected with being his granddaughter, came much, much later.

I discovered Mahler's music by myself at boarding school on a tiny handheld radio at night, in the dark of my dormitory. Later, I went to concerts and came to love Mahler's music greatly. I understand and respect the huge emotion people feel for his music and through this their emotion on meeting me. I do not take this personally but deal with it on another, parallel level of my life – as all lives have many levels of experience and activity.

To look back to childhood when time was not of the essence, is wonderful. Perhaps there's a secret there. Perhaps there is a way that we can look at time differently. Not a stretching out only in front of us in a straight and inexorable line, but as extending out horizontally to each side of us and also far above and far below us.

We are all part of our early memories.

We will always remain so.

Out of this we form our lives.

These memories are our modeling clay, our colours, our petals, our fragrances, our words, and our sounds. Deeply intimate, these early images transform into all the many expressions which can enrich a life - stone figures, musical phrases, structures, families, professions and, more abstractly and elusively, efforts, passions and loves, dreams, and possibilities of all kinds.

Childhood memories can never be damaged, never replaced.

Never believe fate's more than the condensation of childhood.

RAINER MARIA RILKE, 'Seventh Elegy', *Duino Elegies* (1923)

Manners

'Manners are not taught in lessons,' said Alice.

LEWIS CARROLL, *Through the Looking-Glass* (1887)

The best part of sitting is sitting down. People tell you to sit up when you are young. That's stupid.

IVOR CUTLER, BBC4 (February 2003)

Whole Duty of Children

A child should always say what's true,
And speak when he is spoken to,
And behave mannerly at table
At least as far as he is able.

R. L. STEVENSON, *A Child's Garden of Verses* (1885)

'I notice,' said the duck; 'that you talk with only one of your mouths. Can't the other head talk as well?'
   'Oh, yes,' said the pushmi-pullyu. 'But I keep the other mouth for eating – mostly. In that way I can talk while I am eating without being rude. Our people have always been very polite.'

HUGH LOFTING, *The Story of Doctor Dolittle* (1920)

PATTY McARTHUR

At thirteen, my pleasures were few and mostly food-centred. My brothers (three of them) were horrible to me, and there was very little space or peace in our newly built council house on the edge of the Lache estate – a rough area on the outskirts of Chester. Grandma took pride of place in the home - her vital statistics were forty, forty, forty – but then it became too difficult for my mother to look after her and she went to a home for the elderly.

As the only girl in the family, I was allowed to move into her bedroom when she left. At the bottom of the bed, there was an old sea chest used by my mother to store bed linen and materials. While I was supposed to be dusting the bedroom one day, I had a good rummage to the bottom of the chest. I found an old chocolate box full of gorgeous love letters, sloppy poetry, a Sinn Fein badge, and photographs including one of my father (the author of all of the writings to my mother) wearing a dog collar, and signed 'John Moore O.M.I'.

I was found rooting by my mother, severely ticked off, and the evidence was removed to a locked cupboard. It was not until some years later that I learned from an older cousin that my father had been excommunicated from the Catholic church. To fall in love with my mother, a teacher in Preston, Lancashire, while he was a curate working in her parish, caused a huge problem for both of them; and to marry (at a civil ceremony in London, not even in a church) meant that both good Catholics were in mortal sin. They left their native Lancashire under a cloud; Dad taking on boring, mostly clerical work, and mum becoming a mother very quickly. They had a very loving relationship and a hug between the two of them when Dad came home from work could last a good ten minutes!

One of Dad's many one-line sayings was, 'If you don't have a vocational job you should have a vocational hobby'. My father was a much loved man, a great communicator, and kept up his vocation as far as dedicating most of his spare time to the church community and local people. 'Do unto others as you would be done by' was another favourite saying of his, but it didn't always serve me well. It was impossible to avoid confrontations with the rough estate kids when we were 'trespassing' on their territory. As children of an English family living on the Welsh border, we were often verbally insulted by the locals or chased by Welsh farmers (always angry as I recall).

Despite Dad's advice, I did retaliate once when Dolly Waters punched me on the nose giving me a massive nosebleed. She had been yelling obscenities through the window of the school bus, and my friend, Sheila Green, and I turned round to look. 'What d'you think you're staring at?' Dolly Waters said to us. 'Not you!' I had the audacity to answer and with that began a very un-ladylike scrap, which went on after we got off the bus. My younger brother who was with me had been taught never to strike a 'lady' so he wasn't much help but Sheila Green joined in and we nearly got our own back.

When I got home with my ruined hat, three buttons missing from my gabardine coat (which had to last the seven years of secondary school) and in a real mess, I got into even more trouble with my mother. Whenever I was in trouble my mother always believed it was my fault. On another occasion when Barry Shearsmith, who wasn't 'right in the head', weed down my welly, the only sympathy I got from my mother was, 'What were you doing standing near him?'

My brothers constantly got me into trouble back at home – 'Was it your fault, Patty?' my mother would demand. So I would go to meet my Dad off the 6:13 p.m. bus every evening. He liked to go on walks, and I would be his willing companion if ever he asked because Mum was always too busy doing the housework, sewing, gardening, or going to church. The family must all have worn a path going to Mass, benediction, choir practice etc. Somehow, my brothers managed to get out of most of these visits and I would be the one to accompany my father to sing in the choir. Another of my father's sayings was, 'The time you give to God you'll get back a hundred times over'.

Five months before my father died, aged fifty-seven, two papal emissaries came to our house to tell my father that he had been fully restored into the Catholic faith, but he had never left it, and nor would I until I found something better. I seem to be driven, like my father, and like he had, I have too many fingers in too many pies for my own good – even teaching Welsh in a Catholic school! The more you teach, the more you learn.

I'm sure Dad would have appreciated my best one-liner yet that keeps me going in life with my own five children: 'Happiness is a manner of travelling not a state to arrive at.'

Photograph: Ian Horrocks

'That day was very windy. Now have you tried pouring tea and looking at the camera at the same time? Well, I am holding the teapot pouring the tea, and the wind is blowing a gale, and the photographer is saying, "Look at the camera and smile." Then the wind blows down the board advertising Newcastle Brew and a big nail in it stabs Ruud Gullit in the leg. He shot up and screamed, and I thought I had scalded him.' Kathleen Cassidy

KATHLEEN CASSIDY

There were nine of us – four boys and five girls. I was the third one, born in 1927. There was Jimmy, Patsy, and myself. Then there was Eileen, who died as a toddler, Rose, Joan, Vincent, John, and Terry. Seven of us were born in the first house we lived in. It had two rooms, one downstairs and the big bedroom upstairs. The four girls were in one bed. I was happy with that. We went straight out after our tea and stayed out till bedtime.

In the lane we marked out bays with a piece of chalk for games like hopscotch. If you hadn't a piece of chalk, you used a piece of slate. I had a ball on a string that I played against the wall, saying:

Mae West does her best, does her best, does her best
Shirley Temple take a bow, take a bow, take a bow
Betty Grable wasn't able, wasn't able, wasn't able.

I did that for hours. It was a good life. We didn't look for company. We were a very close family. Still are. We had good parents who were devout Catholics. My mother would point to the two holy pictures of our Lady and our Lord on the wall and say, 'Always remember the fourth commandment – Honour thy father and thy mother'. That was drummed into us. We had to live by the rules.

My parents were very strict. There was a time when you

had to be in. I loved music and liked to follow the street singers. People danced in the streets for coppers. One day a children's jazz band started up, and I was away. I marched for miles with the band from Felling-on-Tyne over to Gateshead. Afterwards I was brought back on a wagon and given a little bar of Glaxo chocolate. That was such a luxury it was worth the miles of walking. When I came home, my mother said, 'You see that belt hanging there? I will use it if you follow the band again'. She kept the leather belt on the door as a threat to make us behave. I said, 'All right, I won't.' Well, the next time the band struck up, away I went.

It wasn't until I got back that I remembered my mother's warning. When you are only four, it's easy to forget the fourth commandment. She bathed me and gave me my tea but I knew it was coming because she wasn't a woman who said something she didn't mean. Out came the belt and I really got it on the legs and on the bottom. But the next day she signed me up with Mrs Devonport's jazz club band! Why bother with that slapping? That is the only time I can remember ever being smacked and I am sure there were times I needed it.

I was delicate as a child. I always had the best nighties in case the doctor had to be called! So having asthma had its advantages. My dad was very protective of me because his mother had died young in an asthma attack. If it were raining, he would shout to my mother, 'Now Katy don't let Kathleen go out today. Mind, she has not to go out — it's very damp.' He used to cut out a piece of the flannel blanket, put Vick on it, and make me wear it over my chest and back. There was no treatment for asthma then, no oxygen or inhalers. Sometimes I sat gasping for two hours while the attack came to a height and then went away again.

My mother did the washing at night so that it wouldn't affect my chest. They had it all washed and hung up and dried by morning. Now people touch a button on the washing machine. What a holiday! You can sit and watch a film and have your tea while that's going on! It was washday on a Monday. Ironing day on a Tuesday. The iron had to be put on the fire to warm and go back on again once it was cold. And there was the housework and the windows to do. The steps had to be scrubbed with a grey rubbing stone and the knob of the door polished. The outside had to look good as well. She used to say, 'There's more passes your door than comes in.'

Saturday night was bath night. The water for the tin bath had to be heated in a bucket on the gas. It took for ever because there were so many of us. We were dirtier when we came out! Then to clean our teeth we used a piece of cloth and soot. The toilet – we called it the netty – was in the yard at the back of the house which we shared with the neighbours. There was a string on the back of the door to hold it shut.

My mother was always frightened of us catching germs. Every day she used to give us all a good dose of cod liver oil. Her clothes were stained yellow with the stuff. My brother Jimmy would refuse it but she used to hold his nose until it went down. Afterwards we all got a piece of apple and then we went to school. There was also pink Chemical Food containing vitamins which she trickled over a thick cream called Emulsion. I hated it but if I dodged it, I still got it at bath time.

Rickets was a great worry in those days. Our Rose was in the fever hospital with scarlet fever. Nobody was allowed near her. My mother used to take us up to the grounds where we could wave to her at the window. My mother and I were in the same hospital for several weeks with scarlet fever. Measles was another killer. A cousin came into the house with measles and my little sister Eileen suffered her doom. I can remember the men in high hats taking her out. That's as far back as I can remember. I couldn't have been more than three at the time. There weren't the antibiotics then. My mother used to get the red carbolic soap out and wash the place down.

Before the war, my dad worked at the colliery. There was a shortage of money then even though my dad worked hard. When the dustcarts tipped their load down my dad used to collect the bottles and get money back for them from the shop. All the men did it. They had families to provide for. My dad used to collect up coal duff from the colliery and wet it at home, rolling it up like a snowball for the fire.

We had a big fire with ovens on each side and we needed the coal to stoke the fire to bake the bread. My dad made all the bread for us. It was a heavy job kneading the dough for eight children. He used to put the flour in a big enamel dish in the middle of the floor and say, 'When the devil's in your dad, your dad works hard', as he kneaded the dough.

For breakfast, my dad used to toast the bread on a big pronged-fork on the fire until his face was burning. They made porridge too. My mother used to say porridge put a poultice on your stomach. That would turn anybody off wouldn't it? We never went hungry. On a Monday sometimes mother would send me to the cake shop because the cakes left over from the Saturday were a penny each and I would ask for four stale cakes. She did her best.

One Saturday night, I remember, I was trusted to do the shopping. On the way there was a man standing in the square in a hessian sack tied up in chains. I pushed in to see what was going on there and then I squeezed out again. Then I decided to listen a while to the Salvation Army. I was always drawn to music. This was all on an errand for a dozen eggs, mind. Then I came home along the street and stopped to play Shirley Temple take a bow, take a bow. Aren't they great those games? I forgot I had a dozen eggs in the paper bag. Eggs didn't come in boxes then. When I looked in the bag and saw nothing but gunge I thought I would get killed. Money was short. But my mother didn't touch me. She didn't like to upset me in case it set off an attack of asthma.

I was kept in a lot with the bad chest and once my dad came home with a gramophone and a couple of records. I must have played 'Old Comrades' from eight in the morning to eight at night, and 'The Sun Has Got His Hat On' which was on the other side. I loved music. My mother was a lovely singer, and my father played the harmonica. When Vincent was born, my father would sing 'When I grow too old to dream' with his foot on the rocker of the cradle as he checked his football results.

He used to say to me, 'Pick three draws out', and I always picked Gateshead, Sunderland and Newcastle. 'That's ridiculous,' he would say. 'That will never come up.' But I would insist, 'Put that on.' I loved sport. My father took me with him to cricket matches. He was a great cricketer and was capped for his county.

Just before the war, we moved up to the big four bedroomed house at Windy Nook with a garden at the front and back. My dad used to say wars brought wealth for people. There were Andersen steel shelters to be put in, and the railings round the houses to be taken out to help the war effort. When the war started up, he filled sandbags and then he worked long hours and night shifts in the Royal Ordnance

Factory over in Gateshead where they made shells and guns.

In the blackout you couldn't see your hand turn in front of you. There were big round tin bins in the street billowing out smoke to blacken the place like a fog. You had to grope your way about, that's how dark it was, but you didn't have any fear of somebody tackling you. It was quite safe.

I remember watching a plane coming down. It had caught in one of those barrage balloons and came whizzing down in the street where I was born. Another time, we watched a dog-fight between planes. I had a big yellow streak down my back and was the first one into the air-raid shelter in the garden. Patsy couldn't be bothered to get out of bed! I remember Lord Haw Haw telling us on the wireless that the Germans had hit the Tyne Bridge but it was Spillars, the flour mill, they had hit. They hit the goods station too. There were a lot of air raids. It was rough.

If you went to school without a gas mask you had to go all the way back home to fetch it. The teachers were very hard on children. I thought we were pretty well behaved because we were taught not to answer back. It makes you bitter when you see how the children argue with their teachers now.

We weren't treated delicate at school. It was miles to walk to St John's. I couldn't run because of my asthma and I would be gasping when I arrived. The teacher would say, 'I watched you playing coming down the road. Out with your hand. Out with the other one.' And afterwards, I had to stand out in a corridor with the rain falling on me until the assembly was over.

Mr Duggan was a very bad-tempered man but a good teacher. He used to throw small children over the blackboard and run round to catch them on the other side. This day he wasn't quick enough and he missed the lad. I think he gave him five shillings and said, 'Don't tell your dad because it was an accident.' But the father came down and gave him a hiding.

I am left-handed. The teachers used to force me to write with my right hand and would rap my fingers if I picked up the pen with my left hand. And my mother used to tie my left hand behind my back at mealtimes to stop me cutting the bread with it. Now I peel the potatoes with my right hand, and I do the windows with my left hand and finish off with the right. I am sure it is why I am always in two minds!

Every week we had to take money to school towards the garment we were making. I was making a dress. It was a nightmare. I would say to my mother, 'I can't go to school, I haven't got the money for the dress.' And she would say, 'I will write you a note if you don't want to tell her.' As if that made it any easier! I was made to stand out in the middle of the floor. 'Kathleen,' the teacher would say, 'You didn't bring your tuppence.' But I had to go on sewing the dress. Then when the garments were finished the teacher said, 'Everyone has their dress but you can't have yours because you haven't paid for it.'

My mother always tried to see that we were well turned out. Something was wrong once with the back of my coat and my mother had sewn it in a hurry. At the bell for school, I went to take my coat off and it was sewn to my vest! Those days you wore a vest, a petticoat, a liberty bodice, a cardigan, and a coat. Patsy and I were both crying as she tried to undo it with her teeth because we knew we would both be punished if we were late. She managed it in time.

We had to take our own ingredients for the cookery classes – an ounce of this, that, and the other. It was hard for my mother with more than one girl at school. I will never forget the humiliation. People used to get things on tick. Once, I remember, my mother needed something badly – perhaps two ounces of tea or a quarter of margarine – and she gave me a note to take to the shop. As little as I was, I remember thinking I can't take that note into the shop. I waited until the others came out and then went in. The woman had big boobs which hung over the table. She said, 'Your name will go in the window if you don't get it paid.' That sticks in the mind.

It was a frightening time when you got down with money. There were a lot of children wanting shoes. I remember my mother bought our Jimmy a lovely pair of boots but the lads at school wouldn't let him play football in them because they had to play in their bare feet.

We wore hand-me-downs, but so did everyone. First up, best dressed. I remember knitting myself a pair of knickers and worrying in case I got the plain and pearl loops wrong. When I was fifteen, I knitted myself a bather. I went out into the garden to have a photograph taken. My mother used to tell everybody I was out if I was sunbathing in the garden. If I was looking in the mirror and doing my hair my mother would say, 'You are looking at the mirror that long you will see the devil one of these days.'

In the summer, we used to go by steam train to South Shields on the poor children's trip. Imagine being labelled with that! When you got there you had to stand in a queue to get your hand stamped and a bag of sandwiches. That was to show that you had had your parcel so you couldn't come back and get another one. The stamp was indelible so that it wouldn't come off in the water. Then a few hours after you queued again for another bag and got another stamp on the other hand to show you had had two meals. Like cattle we were. Those stamps were on you for days.

My first job, on the day I was fourteen, was at the Station Hotel. I went into the bar to see Mrs Armistead. I had slides in my hair, a fringe, and white ankle socks. Fourteen was fourteen in those days. She told me I could start as a waitress. I had to wear black silk stockings, black shoes, a white apron and a white lace cap and my hair had to be cut short. I couldn't believe the transformation. And that's how I got started in the catering business.

Now I look after my Pressmen, catering for maybe a hundred of them, on match days at home. The boss – Bobby Robson – comes out on the stage at full time and gives a Press conference about the game. Afterwards, I give him his tea and then I give the visiting manager his tea.

There are three Fs in my life, my faith, my family and my football. Not necessarily in that order on match days! I would never be envious of anybody. I can remember the times when there was nothing. And I mean nothing. You appreciate everything more when you are older when you haven't had any money when you are young. I have all I need. I love my music. And I would still follow the band.

Hard Times

My folks were English . . . We were too poor to be British.
There were so many of us in my family, I was eight years old
before it was my turn in the bathroom. Four of us slept in the
same bed. When we got cold, mother threw on another
brother.

BOB HOPE, *My Life in Jokes* (2003)

Friday January 2nd
BANK HOLIDAY IN SCOTLAND, FULL MOON
I feel rotten today. It's my mother's fault for singing 'My Way'
at two o'clock in the morning at the top of the stairs. Just my
luck to have a mother like her. There is a chance my parents
could be alcoholics. Next year I could be in a children's home.

SUE TOWNSEND, *The Secret Diary of Adrian Mole Aged 13¾* (1982)

Do you remember what it was like to dread the dentist's
drill? Do you remember, as a child, being frightened by the
villain in the pantomime? Being irritated by your nurse?
Hating your cousins? Being made to eat when you felt sick?
Being made to 'lie down' when you wanted to get up and kick
things? And do you remember, worst of all, waking from a
dream to hear, in the next room, your parents quarrelling?

JOHN BETJEMAN, *Evening Standard* (25 August 1934)

She used to shut herself up in the drawing-room when my father came, but one autumn afternoon we were out in the garden and he was giving us a ride in the gardener's handcart. We were all three shouting and thoroughly enjoying ourselves when we came round the corner of the rhododendrons and met my mother, whose self-repression had perhaps relaxed and had released her in the forlorn hope of some sort of reconciliation. Anyhow, there she stood and we all went past her in sudden silence. I have never forgotten the look on her face. It was the first time I had seen life being brutal to someone I loved. But I was helpless. For my father's face had gone blank and obstinate, and the situation, like the handcart, was in his hands. All I could do was to feel miserable about it afterwards and wonder why they couldn't make it up somehow. For I wanted to enjoy my parents simultaneously – not alternately.

SIEGFRIED SASSOON, *The Old Century and Seven More Years* (1938)

These bitter sorrows of childhood! When sorrow is all new and strange, when hope has not yet got wings to fly beyond the days and weeks, and the space from summer to summer seems measureless.

GEORGE ELIOT, *The Mill on the Floss* (1860)

My chief troubles were three – my hair, my hands, and my arithmetic.

E. NESBIT, *Long Ago When I Was Young* (1966)

In the little world in which children have their existence, whosoever brings them up, there is nothing so finely perceived and so finely felt as injustice. It may be only small injustice that the child can be exposed to; but the child is small, and its world is small, and its rocking-horse stands as many hands high, according to scale, as a big-boned Irish hunter.

CHARLES DICKENS, *Great Expectations* (1860–61)

In Stamps the segregation was so complete that most black children didn't really, absolutely know what whites looked like. Other than that they were different, to be dreaded, and in that dread was included the hostility of the powerless against the powerful, the poor against the rich, the worker against the worked for and the ragged against the well dressed.

I remember never believing that whites were really real.

MAYA ANGELOU, *I Know Why the Caged Bird Sings* (1969)

On Guy Fawkes' Day, 1937, eight days after I was born, my mother Truda published an advertisement in the Personal Column of the London *Daily Express* offering me, in effect, to the highest bidder. She specified a date, one week later, when prospective foster parents could attend a kind of private view of the infant. For this unusual ceremony she had selected the Russell Hotel which dominated the east end of Bloomsbury with its lunatic façade – all in all, a happy choice.

DAVID LEITCH, *God Stand Up for Bastards* (1973)

I knew I was an unwanted child when I found that my bath toys included an electric toaster.

JOAN RIVERS, 'Quote Unquote', BBC Radio 4, (16 November 2003)

This be the Verse

They fuck you up, your mum and dad.
They may not mean to, but they do.
They fill you with the faults they had
And add some extra, just for you.

But they were fucked up in their turn
By fools in old-style hats and coats,
Who half the time were soppy stern
And half at one another's throats.

Man hands on misery to man.
It deepens like a coastal shelf.
Get out as early as you can,
And don't have any kids yourself.

PHILIP LARKIN, Collected Poems (1988)

MRS ARBUTHNOT: Don't be deceived, George. Children begin by loving their parents. After a time they judge them. Rarely if ever do they forgive them.

OSCAR WILDE, A Woman of No Importance (1893)

Children's Hour

Between the dark and the daylight,
When the night is beginning to lower,
Comes a pause in the day's occupations,
That is known as the Children's Hour.

HENRY LONGFELLOW, 'The Children's Hour' (1863)

In the High Street, Toytown, stands the Theatre Royal. It is a large and important building; not quite so important as the Town Hall, of course, but still important. The stage-door is in Ark Street, just round the corner, and about this door a group of animals may usually be seen, standing patiently in the hope of seeing some of the marionettes pass in or out.

One morning the waiting animals were surprised to see two unfamiliar figures turn into the stage-door. One was an elderly gentleman with a large hooked nose, and a hump on his back. He wore a frilled collar and carried a heavy stick over his shoulder. He was accompanied by a lady who was evidently his wife. She had a large bundle wrapped in news-paper, and a rather disagreeable-looking baby.

The gentleman stepped inside the stage-door and rapped loudly with his stick on a wooden partition. At once a little shutter behind a pigeon-hole like a booking office window shot up, and out popped the head of Larry the Lamb.

S. G. HULME BEAMAN, *Frightfulness at the Theatre Royal*

FRIGHTFULNESS AT THE THEATRE ROYAL

By

S. G. HULME BEAMAN.

The Original Toytown Story of the famous
Broadcast Play.

The Children's Hour Favourite.

The above characters appear in this Story, they are :

Larry the Lamb, Dennis the Dachshund, The Magician,
Captain Higgins, The Inventor, Mr. Growser, Ernest
the Policeman, The Mayor, The Manager of the Theatre,
Punch, Judy.

Published by
GEORGE LAPWORTH & Co. Ltd., VERNON HOUSE, LONDON, W.C.1

JAN PIEŃKOWSKI

We came to England in November 1946 when I was ten. It was an extremely rough crossing. The boat was pitching and tossing every which way, and just about everybody was sick. My father was in a bad way but my mum and I were not sick. My mum said, 'Let's go and sit up on deck. Nothing is quite so bad out of doors.' We had to go up stairs covered in vomit past grey-faced people clutching at themselves. Once on deck I said, 'It is an island, isn't it?' and my mum answered, 'Yes.' So I knew that if we wanted to leave the island we would have to go through all this misery again, and I said, 'Don't let's go away, let's stay.'

My father was still in the army, in the Polish Second Corps, my mother was in the Polish YMCA. At first we were billeted in a camp just about as far away as you can get from the sea in England, in Foxley, Herefordshire, in a Nissen hut with other Polish families. That winter was terribly cold. Lots of snow. The only source of heat was an iron stove in the middle of the hut. Having had a crash course on England before we arrived, I thought it had a temperate climate and instead it was just like Poland on a really bad day except there were no double windows and all the plumbing was on the outside. That was my first impression of England.

My father then decided that I had to learn English.

It was a lovely spring day when my father took me to Lucton School which was set in the most glorious countryside with rolling hills and big trees, unbelievably English, and not at all like Poland. I remember my father talking to the headmaster, Mr Hodges, in French because his English was not quite up to it then, and asking rather nervously, 'Are there any other foreign boys?' And Mr Hodges said, 'There is one.' My father asked, 'Where does he come from?' And Mr Hodges said, 'Oh, he's Welsh.'

His name was Richards. I can't remember his first name because we all called each other by our surnames. Anyway, Richards became my friend, my only friend. It was not a totally disinterested friendship. Richards collected stamps and he knew we got letters from Poland. He was very nice to me, and I didn't mind that he wanted the stamps.

It was quite tough there and, at the time, I thought I was miserable. I kept on writing to my dad saying, 'Not only have I not learnt a single word of English but I have managed to forget some of the ones I knew already', to try to get him to take me away. But he stuck firm, and I did learn English very fast as a result. Looking back, I don't think that the boys were particularly bad. It was just that I didn't understand their schoolboy culture and I didn't know the language. Once I had learnt English, I was OK.

My mother was stationed in Barnsley, in Yorkshire, running a YMCA club for Polish miners. There was a shortage of miners after the war and the Polish soldiers needed the jobs. So I left Lucton and went to live with my mother in Barnsley. I took the eleven-plus on my own in the town hall because I was changing school at an odd time of the year. I was always changing schools in the middle of a term and having to make friends when other people already had friends.

The town hall was in an imposing classical building at the

top of the high street, and I sat in this rather frightening, large room, all alone. No invigilator. There was one of those awful intelligence tests about a race between sailing boats where *Skylark* gets ahead of *Moonlight* and *Moonlight* has fallen behind another boat, and I had to work out who wins the race. In the end I wrote all the names down on bits of paper – the empirical method – and moved them about because I couldn't do it in my head.

Anyway, I passed. Barnsley Grammar School was at the top of the town surrounded by beautiful moors – a sea of mud, icy wind, bloody knees, that sort of thing. It was another lovely place but in a completely different, rugged, way.

My parents were both demobbed in 1948, and they bought a farm on a hill just by the Welsh border and I went to the local grammar school at Presteigne, an English-speaking town just inside Wales. At the back of the school there were allotments and there was a shed where we used to do woodwork and scripture with Mr Polkinghorne.

The scripture lessons consisted of Mr Polkinghorne reading aloud a thriller and one of the boys standing at the window and telling him if anybody was coming, when he would pick up the Bible and go on with Isaiah. I can tell you now because I am sure he is already reading thrillers to the angels.

At the back of Mr Polkinghorne's shed, there was a railway line and between two particular sleepers there was a gap with a little hollow, and the really bold boys used to lie down, curl up in a ball, and let the train go over them. I had too much imagination. I thought they would just let out the boiling water, or there would be a dangly chain, so I never did it I am ashamed – or glad – to say. That was the dare.

The farm did not succeed and, in 1949, when I was thirteen, we came to London and I went to the Cardinal Vaughan School, a Catholic school. My parents were both working so I was a latchkey child after school and I used to turn on the radio to listen to Uncle Mac and 'Jennings at School', 'Just William', and 'Dick Barton – Special Agent'. Those serials taught me the British way of life. If only I had had 'Jennings at School' when I went to Lucton I would have got on a lot better. I stayed at the Cardinal Vaughan School for four years and, by that time, I was integrated.

People were very friendly on the whole if you said you were Polish. There was a general feeling of warmth and, perhaps more than that, of being allies.

In the offensive of 1939, the Russians and Germans invaded Poland simultaneously from two sides. Then the Germans invaded Russia and they stopped being allies and started fighting each other. This fighting happened in the area round our home, which was in the east of Poland on what would now be the border of Byelo-Russia. My father was a squire, and we lived in a modest Polish manor on a rising bluff by the river Bug. When the fighting started we left the house, the Germans hunkered down in the cellars, and it was shelled to pieces by the Russians across the river. Of the house nothing remains. I have been back a few times. It's a lovely spot. The manor lands were parcelled out under the Communist rule so there are lots of new houses but you can still see how it must have been.

My father got a job at Bromierz doing the admin for a big farm and my mother looked after the house. We lived in a semi-detached staff house and had our own poultry and a piece of the vegetable garden and that is what kept us going. Everything was made at home – the soap, the cheese. You took the flax to a woman who spun it and the yarn to another woman who wove it into cloth. I saw the seasons turning around and the killing of the pig. We were allowed to kill only one pig a year. More than that was punishable by death. It all went to the German front. You were not allowed to make butter. It was like *Sleeping Beauty*, all the butter churns were burned. We did make butter in a metal milk churn with a paddle on a broomstick but it was completely illegal. It was medieval but very interesting for a child. Going to the blacksmith, the fire, and the sparks, that was great.

My mother was very keen that I should have proper healthy food and calcium for bones. So I had to eat carrots which I didn't like at all and I had to drink milk. I liked milk. It came from the cow, all foaming and warm, but I wasn't allowed to drink that milk because of the threat of TB. The milk had to be boiled first and I really hated it.

Our neighbour, the coachman's wife, used to come and babysit and I remember her sitting by the huge grate of the fire with this awful boiled milk. She had this simple idea: she would tell me traditional stories, like the ones the Brothers Grimm collected, terrifying stories of children being chopped up and eaten by *Baba Jaga*, the witch. I was four or five and was absolutely gripped. Then she would stop, just like *Scheherazade*, and say, 'Now drink your milk'. So I had to drink a bit of milk, and then she would go on and there would be another cliffhanger. 'Have some *more* milk.'

I used to have terrible nightmares about the witch. The witch lived in a house on a chicken's foot. For some reason the inside of her house was all made of mirrors. She always used to chase me in my nightmares. You know how you run slower and slower and your feet get bogged down and she's getting closer. And then she puts you in this great pot and then . . .

She was regularly in my nightmares. There was only one lamp and it was on the table in our sitting room where my parents both worked or read at night. I was asleep in the room next door and I could see the light seeping under the door but otherwise it was pitch dark and silent. It was the country. I was terrified of the dark, really scared. I remember the grown-ups' voices coming under the door, and that was very reassuring.

That witch gave birth to *Meg*. Isn't that how you exorcise your terrors, your witch, by turning her into a cosy, incompetent, well-meaning, English sort of witch? *Mr Gumpy* is actually some awful memory from your childhood, John, of this man who goes out in a boat and drowns children. Some babysitter told you this story to keep you quiet!

My father had to leave Bromierz because people were getting arrested all round where we lived and he thought he had better go to Warsaw where you could change your name and identity card. I remember when my father vanished. I was six or seven. He went to a town and he didn't come back. Of course, I wasn't told anything. The coachman who took him came back and gave me a parcel and inside there was a little toy train. I said, 'But where's Daddy?' And my mum said, 'He won't be here for a while.' And I said, 'I don't want a train.'

Anyway, after a bit we went to join him, in the summer of '44. We were in Warsaw when the rising broke out in August. The Russians were advancing closer and closer and the Germans were beginning to withdraw. The Polish underground decided this was our chance to liberate the city, not wait for the Russians, but to do it ourselves. The first few days were impressive – barricades went up in the street, red and white flags appeared everywhere, the swastikas vanished. And then the Germans ceased to retreat because the Russians ceased to advance. The Russians stopped on the other side of the river and waited, and the Germans came back and bombed the place out of existence.

We had a flat on the fifth floor and while there was yet running cold water my mother insisted on going up there every day and giving me a bath. We used to watch the Germans dropping bombs. Somebody suggested to my mother that perhaps she was being rather foolhardy, and she said, 'No, the Germans are a very methodical people. They are not going suddenly to drop a bomb. They are going to do one street, have lunch, come again and do the next street.' There was no anti-aircraft defence so they could do what they pleased. And of course she was right. One day the towers of our parish church and the holy cross just vanished, leaving sky where they had been.

My mother didn't go into the shelters because I did not like crowds of frightened people. The blazing buildings I remember as John Martin pictures. I can't hear the noise. That is very strange. My parents had decided to move to a ruined modern concrete building because they thought the Germans wouldn't waste a bomb on a building that was already ruined. Opposite was a house that had been turned into a hospital with a big red cross painted on the roof. One of those dreadful incendiary bombs like napalm fell on it – everything burnt, the pavement, the trees. My mother put her hands over my ears to stop the screams of the wounded in the hospital. I can't remember hearing any sound at all. I've blotted it out. I can remember the pavement and the trees burning. My father's eyebrows were singed. That I can't remember the noise is perhaps some emotional damage. Even now if I hear somebody screaming it bothers me.

Eventually the city caved in. At the end of the rising, we walked through that part of Warsaw where the walled-off ghetto had been and you would not believe what it was like. It was flat, lumpy terrain with only the gable ends and the chimneys sticking up. Everything else was obliterated.

The surviving population were all gathered together by the Germans in a big railway yard with sheds where the trains were overhauled. We slept in the ditches between the tracks used by the engineers to fiddle around with the undersides of the trains. Although I saw horrendous things, what scared me most was the bad behaviour of some of the civilians – the screaming, the trampling. People would panic saying, 'Gas, gas!'

On the day we were to leave Warsaw, we formed a long queue. The Germans were dividing people up – women and children and old people one side, and able-bodied people the other side – separated by barbed wire. My mother and I were standing about next to the train that we were going to get into and my father was on the other side. My mother shouted at him, 'Jurek!' (George, come over). He ran and vaulted the fence and they shot at him but missed. My mother immediately made him sit under the train and she put some flour on his head to make him look as if he had grey hair. They came and looked in a cursory way but they didn't find him. So we stayed together because of my mother's decisive action.

We were put in open cattle trucks, but it was September and the weather was good, and we were taken to the south of Poland where we were allowed to get out. My parents opted to go to Austria where there was a shortage of people to work on the land. Austria was part of the Reich then so it was all one country. We went to a place called Wetzdorf, just south of Vienna, and my father worked on a big farm and my mother worked in the kitchens of the house. So we had enough to eat during that winter of '44/45.

In the spring, the Russians were coming ever closer. My father, because of his family's experiences, was determined not to get into the Russian empire ever again. There was a mysterious, rather smartly-dressed woman, Frau Wacker, and her teenage son, who did no work at the farm. I think they were Jewish and paid the owner of the farm to keep them. They were also keen to leave so we made our way to Vienna with them and from there caught the train to Munich where we separated. I don't know what happened to them.

It was chaotic. The allies were dropping bombs all over the place and the Germans were beginning to lose their grip. We were on our way to Bavaria and were changing trains at Rosenheim, which was like Crewe Junction, and for some reason both my parents left me on the platform while they went to do something with their papers. A train pulled in and I just started to scream. I was much too old to scream – I was eight – but I shouted with every ounce of strength. My mother came running back and said, 'What ever is the matter?' It was an irrational terror – an animal urge to be together with them. When we were on the cattle trucks leaving Warsaw, I had seen little children being lifted up by the men and passed from car to car because they had lost their family. That had made a big impression on me – the idea of being a lost and helpless child.

We ended up in a beautiful place called Tegernsee, south of Munich, in Bavaria, *Sound of Music* country, on a farm by a lake. The people were pretty fed up with the war and weren't unkind to us. I remember one of the boys threw a stone at me and it hit me on the head but that was the only damage to me all through the war. All the men had gone, even boys went into the army. Anyway, that is where we were in the spring of '45 when the allies came.

I can't say that I, personally, was ill treated by the Germans. My mother lost three close members of her family but I passed through that war as though with some kind of amazing protection. So many children were maimed, or died. I seem to have led a charmed life. I feel like some terrible cheat. These horrible, ghastly things happened all round me but they always happened to other people.

I look back on those years, dare I say it, fondly.

DEVIL'S GALOP
Dick Barton

by CHARLES WILLIAMS
arr. GEORGE BLACKMORE

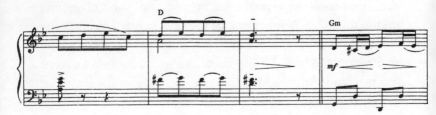

WAR

DICK BARTON

Episode I

PRODUCED BY

NEIL TUSON

(FADE IN SIGNATURE TUNE)

1. ANNOUNCER: Tonight we present the first instalment of a new
Adventure serial. Each evening at this time - Saturdays
and Sundays excepted - we invite you to follow the
exploits of Dick Barton. At the moment, Dick - with an
old wartime comrade - Snowey White - is on holiday at
Grandley - a small village on the Devonshire coast.

(FADE IN FAINT BACKGROUND NOISES SUGGESTIVE OF
THE COAST. SEAGULLS - WAVES, ETC.)

2. DICK: You know Snowey - whoever called this a golf course -
lied in his teeth.

3. SNOWEY: Dunno why you play the game - honest I don't, sir -
(COCKNEY) there don't seem no future in it somehow. Not to me.

4. DICK: Have to take a bit of exercise occasionally.

5. SNOWEY: Should 'a thought it would 'ave been cheaper to buy
some Indian clubs meself. Saved a lot of walkin' too.

6. DICK: I daresay if you got yourself a set of golf clubs you'd
change your mind. There's something about the game
that gets you. Not on this course, though.

7. SNOWEY: There's your ball - in that ridge.

8. DICK: Hell - it's unplayable. And this is supposed to be the
fairway! I shall pick it up Snowey, drop it over my
left shoulder - and play it as though nothing had
happened - without forfeiting a stroke.

9. SNOWEY: You can pick it up an' take it 'ome for me, sir.

10. DICK: You know, Snowey, you must drop this "sir" business.
We're not Captain and sergeant now. We're in civvy
street.

11. SNOWEY: Sorry sir - I can't get used to calling you nothing else
- not now - not after six years.

12. DICK: Well you're a twerp. There - where's the thing gone
now?

13. SNOWEY: (Chuckling) Down a rabbit hole! Here you are. Have
another go. Better still - you turn your back an' I'll
place it for you - comes to the same thing.

14. DICK: (Doubtfully) H'mm - I don't like it, Snowey. T'isn't
cricket!

15. SNOWEY: I know. But it saves a lot of time. There! Now give
it a bash.

16. DICK: Ah - that's better - where's the green? Now the.
Pass me my brassie. No - not that - that one there.
Thanks. My favourite club - brassie. Watch this.

A Bellie Holiday
Picture

BRIAN COX

Our tenement block in Brown Constable Street is still there. I walked past it the other day when I was in Dundee. It is a late Victorian building in brown stone. I used to take joy in flaking the stone away and that's why I am amazed the building is still standing. There was a communal green at the back with a huge pole at the centre of it, as tall as the building, called the 'hing'. This was the washing line for all the inhabitants of our part of Brown Constable Street and Lyon Street who shared the green. In the summer it looked like a great ship in full sail. And beyond the back green was an iron foundry where I used to play as a boy.

The tenement was regarded as slightly upmarket for lower middle class or working class people. My mother had lived in a different part of Dundee, in Wellington Street, where she had just the two rooms. Here, she had the extra room plus the indoor toilet, which was a great facility because most people had outdoor toilets. We had an indoor toilet, but no bath. When my sisters had a bath we used to surround the tin bath with a clotheshorse for modesty's sake. There wasn't a particular bath night in the week. We were Catholic so we didn't have any of those Protestant rules. It was said that the difference between a Catholic and a Protestant household was that when the coal was delivered on a Monday the Catholics would burn it all in the first two days and freeze for the rest of the week, and the Protestants would eke out the bits of coal to last them through the week.

Mr Croal, the coalman, lived above us and he was not popular with my mother. She was quite ill, and obsessive about coal dust. Every time the coal was delivered, she went through this ceremony of stripping off all her clothes down to her petticoat. For some reason she didn't have a corset on, just a petticoat and a pinny. She would cover the place in paper and make the coalman follow a path to the coalbunker which was in an alcove of the kitchen.

The coalbunker in the kitchen was my first stage. This little stage was for performing songs, my party pieces. When I was little, two films came out, *The Jolson Story* and *Jolson Sings Again*, which were very popular. My great act, as a three-year-old, was to do Al Jolson impersonations. I learnt to read by recognising the names of the singers on records so I could look at records when I was very little and say, 'This is Frank Sinatra singing *Young at Heart*, this Vaughan Monroe, this is Perry Como.' My sister used to get pissed off with me because I broke a few records in my time. We used to sing for our party pieces. New Year was a big celebration. My mother would be up at four o'clock in the morning making steak pie in her dressing gown for people sitting drunk as skunks having bevvied from five o'clock the previous day.

Off the kitchen, there was a tiny wee scullery where my mother cooked. Once, my brother, father and I were home and she had a terrible accident cooking the chips for our tea. She was angry and distracted by my brother and she hit this pan of boiling fat which went all over her arm. It was horrific, and she passed out immediately. Her arm was like lemon meringue pie, I remember it vividly.

In the kitchen there was a second alcove with a bed, where my brother and I slept, and a mother of pearl crucifix on the wall. It looked like a little chapel. I used to pretend to be a priest and do the Mass bouncing down the bed. The priest would come to visit us, and also the nuns who looked like huge white swans in those white headdresses. My mother would berate the canon of the parish, a man called Canon McKinley after Mass on Sunday. She called him Canon Cash because he was always asking for money. She was quite fierce and she used to say to him, 'How dare you ask for money from people who have just been through a horrific war and who have no money.' Little Canon McKinley would try to avoid her outside the church.

Next to St Patrick's Church was the Broadway cinema and diagonally opposite to the iron foundry was the Royal cinema. The Royal building is still there but, alas, both the cinemas have gone. I saw James Dean in *Giant*, Marlon Brando in *On the Waterfront*, Jerry Lewis, Spencer Tracey, lots of films. Double features were prevalent in the Fifties. There would be one double feature on Monday, Tuesday and Wednesday, and a second double feature on Thursday, Friday and Saturday. So I would often see eight films a week. The cinema was my baby-minder. I started going on my own when I was six for I was very adventurous by then. I would fall asleep and slip off the chair on to the floor. On more than one occasion I woke up in the early hours of the morning wondering where I was, and had to break out of the cinema.

It was great. There was a nice atmosphere at home. Inside the front door there was a lobby, quite a big space where I used to play. There was a big photograph on the wall of my maternal grandfather, a drill sergeant called Sergeant James McCann, which used to frighten me. He had a big barrel chest, which I have inherited, and red hair, and wore the full kilt and beevor. The other family photographs were kept in a pink, square toffee tin in the press in the lobby.

The press was where my mother stored her holy water from Lourdes. It smelled foul. I think my mother brought back the whole font of Lourdes. She went to Lourdes in times of domestic crisis, once in 1936, and again in 1953 with my father two years before he died, when they brought back more of the water. The 1953 water wasn't as foul smelling as the 1936 lot which, by that time, had been around for fifteen years. My parents went through difficult periods. After the war, my mother was really quite ill and one time she ran away. She was institutionalised after my father died, following a severe mental breakdown.

My father died when I was nine. He was a very gentle man. He used to run a little grocery shop in a ghetto area of Dundee down in the centre of town called Charles Street. He was very generous, my father, and helped to organise and supply some goods for a Coronation party in Charles Street for Queen Elizabeth and for another one in our local street.

Two years after my father died, we moved to a modern corporation house – a council house with a bathroom. The old house held too many memories for my mother. It was a shame because I loved that 'hoose' in Brown Constable Street.

Books

Listen, my children, and you shall hear
Of the midnight ride of Paul Revere,
On the eighteenth of April in Seventy-five.

HENRY LONGFELLOW, from *Paul Revere's Ride* (1861)

I remember distinctly the suddenness with which a key turned in the lock and I found I could read – not just the sentences in a reading book with the syllables coupled like railway carriages, but a real book. It was paper-covered with the picture of a boy, bound and gagged, dangling at the end of a rope inside a well with the water rising above his waist – an adventure of Dixon Brett, detective. All a long summer holiday I kept my secret, as I believed: I didn't want anybody to know that I could read. I suppose I half consciously realised even then that this was the dangerous moment.

GRAHAM GREENE, 'The Lost Childhood', *Collected Essays* (1969)

I told him that I had just read a book by Bernard Shaw. My father stopped still in the path where we were walking and said: 'I have heard of other people having children like that, but I have always prayed God I might be spared.'

STEPHEN SPENDER, *The Old School*, ed. Graham Greene (1934)

I cannot remember learning to read, but my father gave me on my fourth birthday a copy of *Robinson Crusoe* as a reward for having myself read it from end to end . . . Whenever we were not out of doors we were reading or listening to my mother reading aloud. Fortunately for us my mother enjoyed this and read extremely well. For one thing, she would never read aloud to us a book that she did not enjoy reading to herself. This simple rule, which should be observed by all mothers who read aloud (and I am sorry for the children of mothers who do not), saved us from a deal of rubbish. Any book worth reading by children is also worth reading by grown-up persons.

ARTHUR RANSOME, *The Autobiography of Arthur Ransome* (1976)

And when the Arthur Ransome books found their way to the Express Bookshop in Cairo I became infatuated, addicted. I saved up my pocket money to buy them as they arrived – objects so covetable as to be awesome, those green bindings with the gold lettering, and the distinctive dust-jackets. I read them like some awestruck peasant, gawping at the goings-on of these incredible children: their airy confidence, their sophistication, their independence. The narratives patently bore no relation to real life, but were enthralling as pure fantasy. And then there was the matter of the ambience, this exotic landscape of hills and lakes and greenery and rain and boats and peculiar birds and animals. From time to time I would lift my eyes from the page to look out at my own humdrum environment of palms and donkeys and camels and the hoopoe stabbing the lawn.

PENELOPE LIVELY, *Oleander, Jacaranda* (1994)

I was six or so when *The Ugly Duckling* aroused in me the melancholy of life, gave me to see the deep sadness which pervades all romance, beauty, and adventure. I laughed heartily at the old hen-bird's wise remark that the world extended past the next field and much further; I could perceive the humour of that. But when the ugly duckling at last flew away on his strong pinions, and when he met the swans and was accepted as an equal, then I felt sorrowful, agreeably sorrowful. It seemed to me that nothing could undo, atone for, the grief and humiliations of the false duckling's early youth. I brooded over the injustice of his misfortunes for days, and the swans who welcomed him struck me as proud, cold, and supercilious in their politeness. I have never read *The Ugly Duckling* since those days. It survives in my memory as a long and complex narrative, crowded with vague and mysterious allusions, and wet with the tears of things.

ARNOLD BENNETT, *The Truth About an Author* (1903)

'Nuffing ever happens to me,' muttered Jim to himself. He said this, half in anger and half as a kind of challenge; had not the heroes in *The Young Explorer* and *The Boy Aviators* said just the same thing and had not adventures by the dozen immediately befallen them?

However, nothing *did* happen to Jim. He got up, ate, went to school, was good or naughty as the mood took him, stood about hoping for adventures, 'despaired' like the heroes of his books (though what this meant he was never quite sure), read more books from the Public Library, ran errands, went to bed, and got up and began all over again; *still* nothing whatever out of the common occurred.

'I'm fed up,' said Jim . . . 'Nuffing ever happens like in books.'

EVE GARNETT, *The Family from One End Street* (1937)

They were all very hungry at lunch time. They went back up the cliff-path, hoping there would be lots to eat – and there was! Cold meat and salad, plum-pie and custard, and cheese afterwards. How the children tucked in!

'What are you going to do this afternoon?' asked George's mother.

'George is going to take us out in a boat to see the wreck on the other side of the island,' said Anne.

ENID BLYTON, *Five on a Treasure Island* (1942)

Though I liked reading (and showed off at it), it was soon borne in upon me that the world of books was only distantly related to the world in which I lived. The families I read about were not like our family (no family ever quite was). These families had dogs and gardens and lived in country towns equipped with thatched cottages and mill-streams, where the children had adventures, saved lives, caught villains, and found treasure before coming home, tired but happy, to eat sumptuous teas off chequered tablecloths in low-beamed parlours presided over by comfortable pipe-smoking fathers and gentle aproned mothers, who were invariably referred to as Mummy and Daddy . . .

Had it been only stories that didn't measure up to the world it wouldn't have been so bad. But it wasn't only fiction that was fiction. Fact too was fiction, as textbooks seemed to bear no more relation to the real world than did the story-books.

At school or in my *Boy's Book of the Universe* I read of the minor wonders of nature – the sticklebacks that haunted the most ordinary pond, the newts and toads said to lurk under every stone, and the dragonflies that flitted over the dappled surface. Not, so far as I could see, in Leeds.

ALAN BENNETT, *Writing Home* (1994)

The Public Library

Every Saturday I used to go up to the public library to get two books. One would be about the current affairs of the day – it might have been biography, it might have been about politics – and one would have been perhaps a novel for my mother. Every single Saturday. And the librarian knew I would come.

MARGARET THATCHER, *Maggie: The First Lady*, ITV1 (6 March 2003)

'Got any books on hawks, missis?'

The girl behind the counter looked up from sorting colourless tickets in a tray.

'Hawks?'

'I want a book on falconry.'

'I'm not sure, you'd better try ornithology.'

'What's that?'

'Under zoology.'

She leaned over the desk and pointed down a corridor of shelves, then stopped and looked Billy over.

'Are you a member?'

'What do you mean, a member?'

'A member of the library.'

Billy pressed a finger into the ink pad on the desk and inspected the purple graining on the tip.

'I don't know owt about that. I just want to lend a book on falconry, that's all.'

'You can't borrow books unless you're a member.'

BARRY HINES, *A Kestral for a Knave* (1968)

As I walked past the statue of Joan of Arc, I always remembered my grandmother's joke, the first time she took me to visit the Art Gallery, which used to be housed in the same building.

'What's Joan of Arc made of?' she asked.

'Bronze?' I ventured.

'Orleans!' she yelled and hooted with laughter.

Through the revolving door I'd go, out of the blue-white blaze of the sun into mahogany, pietra dura and green baize. I strode confidently, hoping no one would challenge me for being no more than fourteen. My fears of discovery were probably unfounded; my face was so grey and drawn with adolescent misery, that the average bar-tender in any of the lavatorial pubs that lined Swanston Street would probably have poured me a brandy without missing a beat, judging me nearer thirty than twenty. I'd take the staircase in a busy little tripping run, as if I did it twenty times a day, and stroll loftily into the reading room. Convinced, as all adolescents are, that everyone was looking at me, I dared not stop and peer. Too proud to hiss a question and scared that my question might give me away, I never quite got the hang of the system.

As in the British Museum, the circular reading room was domed in glass, with long tables radiating from a mahogany core towards the book-lined walls ... Although the supervisor in his pulpit at the hub worked at some librarianly task without raising his head, I was sure he kept a fingertip on each spoke like a spider. I knew that if I should dare to chew or fart or drop a book, or blot it with my cheap pen, he would dart down and paralyse me. So I would quickly get a book, which was never quite the book I wanted, edge my behind on to a slippery chair, and take notes the way I saw others doing. So the habit of a lifetime was formed.

GERMAINE GREER, *Daddy, We Hardly Knew You* (1989)

CORNELIA BATHURST

I spent most of my childhood in a series of kilts because my mother reckoned kilts were interchangeable between boys and girls. Nowadays, of course, jeans would do. As the youngest of six children, I wore the kilts at the bottom of the pile. I liked them very much because they had frayed and frilly edges. I thought that gave them a certain cachet. They were McPherson tartan, grey with a bit of red. We have a perfectly good tartan, the Macdonald, which is green, but my mother preferred the McPherson. And there was one Lindsay tartan kilt I was particularly fond of because it was a faded green and crimson, and very frayed. So that was my childhood uniform - kilt, my brothers' prep school grey jerseys, and black Wellington boots.

I lived in two places. I lived in a cottage at the end of a drive with a retired nanny. It was charming but the coldest house I have ever been in because it had five outside walls. Then one went up the drive to the family home. This was a Victorian house with rooms like a cathedral. It must have had state-of-the-art central heating put in at some point but only a whisper of warmth came through the iron gratings. The only time I remember being warm was when my father, who used to sit to the left of the fire, would throw the company reports he had finished reading on to the fire and there was a wonderful 'hrumph' as the chimney was set alight, and then the room was quite warm for a while.

The fire had a club fender entirely of brass, nothing upholstered, with a corner to sit on at each end. My mother, who had been to a French school and could sit on three inches of any chair, would sit bolt upright at one end and my eldest sister hogged the other end. The middle of the fender was known as the crow's seat because of the family's habit of perching on it like crows on a line. Not surprisingly, everyone competed for this hardish perch. It took two and half people, which meant that anyone else further down in the pecking order just froze on the outside. As the runt of the litter, I was in perpetual outer darkness.

The only one who had it taped was the white bull terrier, Bulla, who would squeeze through the bars of the fender and there he lay between the fender and the fire until all his shell-pink bits went lobster pink. At which point he would get up very slowly and totter off to the other side of the room and crash to the floor making all the china rattle in the cupboard. Bulla was my very great friend, a lovely character. I was taking samples of hair one day and cut a square end to his tail. The family tried to get me to own up – in vain – but I was eventually caught when a cluster of rigid white prickles was found in a small tin amongst the curls of a Victorian locket collection.

During the Second World War, most of the house was put under dustsheets ready for conversion to a hospital and several iron beds were moved in. And the nursery part of the house was turned over to the evacuees. There were twenty-eight evacuees altogether, and they came from Glasgow. I don't remember the adults but there were various children called Bridie and Queenie, and names like that. For me, it was heaven on earth to have new friends. But it didn't last very long because the mothers fought with one another, said it was too quiet in the country, and returned to Glasgow with all the children. I was really sorry.

There was a Polish regiment camped on the edge of the village. My parents furnished the dining room of the house as a drawing room for the officers and made a bathroom for their use. I remember the red and white flash on their collars. Life at home was very quiet and so an influx of Polish officers was heavenly, especially for my oldest sister. One of them I remember sat down and gave a glorious concert at the piano in amongst the dustsheets. So many of them, I now realise, must have gone back to fight and have been killed.

My war effort was to keep some ducks. A duck house was put into the garden of Nanny's cottage and we collected six Khaki-Campbell ducks. I was supposed to write down in a little black notebook how many eggs the ducks laid every day but, very quickly, the ducks disappeared down to the burn that ran through the village. Then the eggs dried up until, one day, one hundred and twenty eggs were discovered under the duck house. The number of eggs doubtless has grown in the telling. Eventually, Nanny took over the care of the ducks.

Nanny was wonderful, a human form of Mrs Tiggywinkle. She came to the family when my eldest brother was six weeks

old, and she stayed for the other children and was retired in the cottage. She had an extraordinary gift for making everything she touched live; she made children live, but plants in particular. She never went anywhere, not even to the local town three miles away. Everything she wanted was delivered by the vans that came past.

To begin with, my two siblings nearest me in age also lived in the cottage but they were taken up to the house when they became ill with some childhood disease. One was prone to every disease; I caught ringworm from the ponies, impetigo from the evacuees. It was all part of childhood. I was eighteen by the time I was moved up into the big house. Perhaps one of the servants' rooms had become free.

When I was thirteen, I was allowed to come up to the house for dinner. Everybody changed for dinner. My father used to change into a dinner jacket every night. I can remember the conversation going above my head like a cloud. One could look up at the cloud or let it float by. There was a lot of talk about crankshafts amongst my brothers around the dining-room table. And all my family were botanists so they talked about the lesser-spotted something orchid or Hooker's duck-weed. None of this seemed very relevant to one's life. After dinner, one of my brothers would be detailed to take me down to Nanny's cottage, which they were always trying to dodge.

My brothers were very kind to me but I was pretty useless to them and got in their way. The moments one was included were wonderful and one was prepared to do almost anything to join in their games. My aunt, who was a seventh child, said she was going to start a runts club for the youngest members of large families and the motto would be, Wait for Me.

When my brother, who is eight years older, was about to go to prep school he handed me his bear called Nutty and asked me to look after him. I adored Nutty, and he went everywhere with me, but at some point I thought Nutty would look better without ears and I removed them. They were lost for about two years until they were discovered in a weaving-set and sown back on to Nutty's head. I still have Nutty. His nose is prickly where someone shaved it with a pair of scissors.

Wait for Me. There was a lovely garden but we did not play in it. We played in what would be called in Scotland the policies, the area round about the house. My siblings were living up at the big house and so to some extent were apart. As the youngest, I was left to do what I wanted. So I spent most of my time in the woods and the village, making up games, usually accompanied by Bulla.

A lot of time was spent in church. It was a beautiful church, very austere and white. Church of Scotland. It had the Ten Commandments written in black Gothic lettering on Gothic plaques with all references to God picked out in red. 'For I the

Lord thy God am a jealous God.' We sat in the front of the top gallery, in perfect range for reading them. When I go there now I test whether I can still read them. Thou shalt not kill. Thou shalt not commit adultery. Thou shalt not steal. One can cheat with those three. But the one about graven images, which is my favourite, is more difficult to remember and therefore I have to try and read it. I like the bit about the sins of the fathers being visited on the children until the third and fourth generation. Such beautiful language.

There was quite a lot of time to be passed during the church services so most of the church's not-quite-square features are burnt into my memory. As well as listening to the sermon, there were other occupations. If I stared hard enough at the minister in his pine pulpit I could make an aura of yellow appear round his black robe and bald head and pretend it was gold. I could follow the progress of a slater (wood louse) along the match-board pew front, up the church hymnary, down the Psalter and into the corner groove. I could idle away a minute or more on how I might tip a very small hymn book over the front of the pew on to the heads below and what I would say to deny it. Or there were the names of the hymn writers to be thought about. John Bacchus Dykes, Sabine Baring-Gould, Augustus Montagu Toplady, Verantius Honorious Clement-ianus Fortunatus (AD 530–609), etc.

We had a Scottish governess who taught me the Books of the Old Testament. Together with adding by rote, I learnt the order of the Books, in fours: Genesis, Exodus, Leviticus, Numbers. Deuteronomy, Joshua, Judges, Ruth. Somewhere around Obadiah I went to pieces, and still do. When we were doing lessons in the dining room the governess would disappear for elevenses with my mother. They were best of friends. Meanwhile one was getting up to no good taking the knives out of the drawers, which were very sharp, and experimenting on the furniture.

One of my mother's skills was to fill the house with flowers. There was a lovely walled garden in the Scottish manner which is to grow the vegetables and the flowers all together, the flowers on the outside and the vegetables in the middle – rows of lovely cabbages, cauliflowers, and curly kale. My mother must have been well in advance of her time for she grew all sorts of unusual vegetables too that are now coming into fashion. One was what she called sugar peas, *mange-tout*, and another was kohlrabi.

It was such a different era. She set great store by the quality of the linen, and must have given an extraordinary amount of time to the linen cupboard. All the sheets – linen of course – had the initials of my mother's maiden name, date, and number in the batch embroidered into the top left-hand corner. A sheet was a sheet, one would think, but there was a whole world to do with the quality of the linen, how it was woven, where it came from, which is completely lost now. And the amount of time that went into ironing damask napkins and the rest, all completely gone. There is something rather satisfying about ironing a damask napkin because it is so beautiful.

These ways belonged to an older generation. My mother and father were more like grandparents. My father was born in 1880 and did not get married until he was forty-five, and then he had six children. So I had a very old-fashioned upbringing. That Victorian house had an indoor staff of five people even after the war. There was a cook, a housemaid, a table maid, and an under table maid and an under housemaid. Servants waited on servants because the whole structure of service was so embedded.

My father was heavily involved in the country's steel supplies and during the war travelled up and down to London all the time. As a director of the LNER railways, he had a travel pass, like a medal. Occasionally he would pull this beautiful clanking object out of his pocket. There were four medals, one for each of the four railways, the LNER, LMS, GWR and Southern Railways, and another one for the London Underground.

At that time the locomotives were named after the directors. So the fun for me when I went to boarding school was to race to the front of the train to see if I had been pulled by the Andrew K McCosh. The beautiful blue locomotive has gone, but we do still have the plate with my father's name on it.

We used to go on holidays to a place called Elie, in Fife. It took five changes by train to get there, which must have been a nightmare for the grown-ups but was enormous fun for children. The great excitement after you had made it to Edinburgh was crossing the Forth Bridge. Magic for a child. Then there was another change at Thornton Junction past Kilconquhar – pronounced Kill-conk-her by my brothers with accompanying gestures until finally we burst on the landscape of Elie.

In the early days we – that is, Nanny, another nurse, my sister and brother (the two siblings nearest to me in age) – would go to a little house called Allanton which had green windows and a sandy garden, down by the breakwater, and the parents would go to the Marine Hotel, and never the twain would meet! In those days it was easy to be rid of your children. We went down to the beach in those extraordinary bloomers that we hitched up over our dresses.

I am surprised that my parents felt it necessary to take us all that way for holidays when we lived in the middle of the country. There were all sorts of walks as a child. When one was nine or ten, as a beater for the grouse shooting. This was hard walking, nearly all at forty-five degrees on burnt heather, which is horrible to walk on. But one was compensated by the beauty of the place and the untold sum of ten shillings for a day's beating. Hill walking is a great pleasure to this day – it is in the blood. And I can remember walks in the snow with the white bull terrier. My brother would pick Bulla up and, as an experiment, throw him into the snowdrifts to see if he made a dog-shaped hole.

Later holidays were spent botanising, which usually meant wandering about in the rain with your head down looking for duckweeds in a muddy pond. That wasn't terribly exciting, so I spent most of the time curled up on the bed reading something like *Forever Amber*. We went to Portpatrick and Wigtonshire, any place that was famous for wild flowers. We each had a small book called *Illustrations of the British Flora* by Bentham and Hooker with accurate line engravings, four to a page, of the entire flora. When we found a new plant, we painted it into the book using the tiny water-colour box we carried with our Bentham. So it was a competitive family game.

A tremendous amount of my childhood was spent free-wheeling. I feel so privileged to have had that degree of freedom. Apart from the lessons with the governess, we spent untold hours on our own. Two girls came to live in the next-door house and we spent whole days riding all over the place on our bicycles. It would be unthinkable today, with the traffic the way it is, to let children ride about in the same way. So I am saddened that children no longer can have that freedom. Nothing for the imagination.

Place

'I've explored places where no white man ever set his feet before,' said William.

RICHMAL CROMPTON, *William – In Trouble* (1927)

I can call it all back and make it as real as ever it was, and as blessed. I can call back the prairie, and its loneliness and peace, and a vast hawk hanging motionless in the sky, with his wings spread wide and the blue of the vault showing through the fringe of their end feathers. I can see the woods in their autumn dress, the oaks purple, the hickories washed with gold, the maples and the sumachs luminous with crimson fires, and I can hear the rustle made by the fallen leaves as we ploughed through them. I can see the blue clusters of wild grapes hanging from the foliage of the saplings, and I remember the taste of them and the smell. I know how the wild blackberries looked, and how they tasted, and the same with the pawpaws, the hazelnuts, and the persimmons; and I can feel the thumping rain, upon my head, of hickory nuts and walnuts when we were out in the frosty dawn to scramble for them with the pigs, and the gusts of wind loosed them and sent them down.

MARK TWAIN, *Mark Twain's Autobiography* (1925)

No one was coming. No one ever did come, it seemed, and she took another long breath, because she could not help it, and she pushed back the swinging curtain of ivy and pushed back the door which opened slowly – slowly.

Then she slipped through it, and shut it behind her, and stood with her back against it, looking about her and breathing quite fast with excitement, and wonder, and delight.

She was standing *inside* the secret garden.

FRANCES HODGSON BURNETT, *The Secret Garden* (1911)

The early part of the day was devoted to the walled garden. Its door opened with a rising shriek, and from the time it took to announce that it had shut, you knew, even if you couldn't see whether more than one person had come into it. If you were there first, you could hide behind a clump of flowers or one of the upturned millstones that stood at intervals along the terrace. Sometimes, without being seen, I could get as far as the shed, filled with broken and discarded objects blanketed with spider's web. Flower-pots, still containing earth, bulbs, a dibber, a rusty trowel, a few roorkie chairs and a pile of little pieces of coloured glass, intended for making mosaics. Apart from their colour, their grainy, semi-translucent texture fascinated me: I wanted to know them, and therefore to eat them – but was prevented.

Then there was the profusion of flowers, many of which, when picked and turned upside down, could be transformed into gorgeous princesses with a dazzling change of wardrobe. Throughout the summer, many hundreds of these were abandoned, left to wilt in a corner of the garden.

ANGELICA GARNETT, *Deceived with Kindness* (1984)

He took one last look at the Blind Pool. It was the loveliest thing he had seen so far in the forest, and he had enjoyed this day more than any other they had had so far.

He did not know then that years afterwards he would remember that picture; the dark pool set among the trees, so still, so calm, starred with those wax-like lilies, and the grey heron sitting on the log. Some things we see pass out of the mind, or, at least, are forgotten; others, little things, little glimpses such as this never depart. And the memory of that first view of the Blind Pool would still be in his mind forty years afterwards, rather faded perhaps, like an old photograph in an album, but still there, an imperishable masterpiece.

B.B. *Brendon Chase* (1944)

One must remember that in the early days of this century England was a quiet country. The only sounds in the countryside then were the *tink-tink* of the blacksmith's forge, a sound which I heard so many times while sitting on the swing under the great cedar at home; the measured *clip-clop* of horses' hooves, the barking of dogs, bleating of sheep and, of course, in the autumn the low, fat hum, rising and falling, of the threshing machines, busy in the rickyards.

B.B. *A Child Alone* (1978)

DEBORAH MOGGACH

This is a story about me and horses, and how I realised that writing could both lie and tell the truth. As a girl I was pony-mad (actually I still am). I had a real pony called Wally – a piebald mare who I passionately loved. We had a cottage in the New Forest and I rode her all weekend, each weekend, and all through the holidays. We swam together in flooded gravel pits; I sat on her for hours while she grazed, sitting back to front and using her rump as a table to prop up my book.

During the week, however, we were separated. From Monday to Friday I lived in London and during this time Wally mutated into a fantasy horse, fused into me. I used to neigh and whinny around the streets of Camden Town, tethering myself to railings when I went into shops. This me-horse didn't resemble Wally at all; she was much more biddable than the stroppy, off-hand creature who blundered into me, trod on my feet and didn't love me the way I loved her. She was the true horse of my dreams, sensitive, beautiful and, of course, doing exactly what I told her to do. Easy, as she was me. Both coexisted happily, just as a marriage can have room for a fantasy pin-up. And the two were sort of linked; sometimes I even brought horse-nuts to school in my pocket and sniffed them during lessons.

My mother drew horses brilliantly and used to illustrate children's books, specialising in the pony stories of writers like the Pullein-Thompson sisters. She also started writing books herself – picture books and stories for older children.

Sometimes Wally would make an appearance in her plots. My piebald mare was transmuted again, a fictional pony taking part in other people's adventures. This was thrilling, of course, and also slightly disorientating. Now I'm grown up and write novels myself I'm used to doing this, but back then I had my first insight into the way stories draw another truth out of what's laughingly known as Real Life. Having written about events in the past, I've found that my memories have a sort of hologram hovering over them, overlaying and altering what actually happened.

One day, when I was twelve, I was riding through the forest when I spotted what looked like a rusting iron pineapple. I must have reported it because I remember returning to the scene and finding police tape strung around it. The next week, in the local paper, I read a paragraph which began with the words: 'Mr J Howe, of Little Patch, Munstead, found an unexploded bomb on Thursday . . .'

This was my first realisation that maybe one should trust fiction rather than fact. The truth being: 'Miss D Hough, of Little Thatch, Minstead . . .' They'd even got my sex wrong.

Or maybe it was the beginning of another lesson: don't trust what you read in the papers.

Pets

He was very fond of animals and kept many kinds of pets. Besides the goldfish in the pond at the bottom of his garden, he had rabbits in the pantry, white mice in his piano, a squirrel in the linen closet, and a hedgehog in the cellar. He had a cow with a calf too and an old lame horse – twenty five years of age – and chickens and pigeons and two lambs and many other animals. But his favourite pets were Dab-Dab, the duck; Jip, the dog; Gub-Gub, the baby pig; Polynesia, the parrot; and the owl, Too-Too.

HUGH LOFTING, *The Stories of Doctor Dolittle* (1920)

One of the nicest things about my young life was my mice. After breakfast I changed into my mouse frock or perhaps pinafore – dark blue it was – and the darling silky mice came out of their cage and wandered over me: I don't know how or why we communicated but presumably we did. Sometimes the mice climbed down me on to the floor and I after them. How pleasing and how large things are from underneath!

NAOMI MITCHISON, *Small Talk* (1973)

There were four family dogs to play with besides my own special and beloved bull-terrier, whom I had named Jou-Jou, somewhat inappropriately, considering the size to which he grew. In winter evenings all the dogs used to lie in a sort of doggy carpet before the big hall fire, with me generally stretched out in their midst with my head on Jou-Jou's side, while Papa and Mama grumbled that they would like a bit of fire too.

GRACE LOVAT FRASER, *In the Days of My Youth* (1970)

The rabbit has a charming face,
Its private life is a disgrace.
I really dare not name to you
The awful things that rabbits do.

ANON

He was christened Adolf. We were enchanted by him. We
couldn't really love him, because he was wild and loveless to
the end. But he was an unmixed delight. We decided he was
too small to live in a hutch – he must live at large in the house.
My mother protested, but in vain. He was so tiny. We had him
upstairs, and he dropped his tiny pills on the bed and we were
enchanted.

Adolf made himself instantly at home. He had the run of the house, and was perfectly happy, with his tunnels and his holes behind the furniture.

We loved him to take meals with us. He would sit on the table humping his back, sipping his milk, shaking his whiskers and his tender ears, hopping off and hobbling back to his saucer, with an air of supreme unconcern. Suddenly he was alert. He hobbled a few tiny paces, and reared up inquisitively at the sugar basin. He fluttered his tiny fore-paws, and then reached and laid them on the edge of the basin, whilst he craned his thin neck and peeped in. He trembled his whiskers at the sugar, then did his best to lift down a lump.

'*Do* you think I will have it! Animals in the sugar pot!' cried my mother, with a rap of her hand on the table.

D. H. LAWRENCE 'Adolf', *Phoenix: The Posthumous Papers of D. H. Lawrence* (1936)

PENELOPE LIVELY

In my grandmother's garden there was an eighteenth-century lead fish tank. It was about three feet high – nicely child-height – and was surmounted by a statue of a boy with a dolphin under one arm. Within the tank were goldfish, which could just be seen cruising down at the bottom in the murky depths, little glints of gold. At one side there was a metal lever, which operated a mechanism to drain the tank, when required.

When I was six, I pulled that lever. I know that I was six because I spent my childhood in Egypt and the year in which we came to England, and spent the summer at my grand-mother's house, was 1939, when I was six. Alone with the fish tank, no adult in sight, I peered down at the goldfish, and then my hand was drawn irresistibly to the lever. I'm not sure that I knew what its function was, but I soon found out. There was a glug, a gurgle, and I watched with horror as the water level began rapidly to fall.

I rushed into the house. I said that I felt ill. I had a pain. I was not at all well. I was put to bed, cosseted. And lay there experiencing my first serious, debilitating onset of guilt. In the event, someone discovered the gasping goldfish in time; all was well. Except for me, pole-axed by that fearful emotion; I can remember the feeling to this day.

Later that summer, in September, the household was summoned to sit beside the wireless and listen in silence to a thin, dry man's voice. I remember that too, very well, and that I wondered why they were all so solemn, and what a war was. A few weeks later, we went back to Egypt, and in the years after that I discovered, as the Libyan campaign raged in the desert, not too far away.

YORAM GROSS

John, dear old friend, I will tell you how I communicated with a young mouse.

It was during the Second World War when, as a Jew, I had to hide from the Nazis. This time I was hiding in an attic. Mrs Grabovska, a distinguished Polish lady who hated the Nazis, gave me shelter and did her best to help me survive. Every morning she gave me a piece of bread and tea, and the same again for lunch. Mrs Grabovska had only the same food for herself. She was looking after her two little girls on her own because her husband, a Polish officer, was in prison.

I kept very quiet, so as not to draw the attention of the unfriendly neighbours. The only noises that could be heard from time to time were the sounds of mice squeaking but then the neighbours used mousetraps to stop that. So at night, after soup and maybe a scrap of bacon that Mrs Grabovska would bring me, I kept very still, not making any sound.

One night, lying in my hideout on some straw, ready to sleep, I heard noises. I opened one eye and realised I was not alone. There was another soul hiding with me. Although not a Jew, a tiny grey mouse also had a reason to hide. It was not aware of my presence because I was keeping very still. The poor creature was searching for food and, after looking around and finding nothing, it disappeared. I was left by myself, lonely again.

Next day, when Mrs Grabovska brought my food, I left a

tiny bit for my partner. Maybe the little mouse would come again. If we shared the same space, we should share also the food. I was right. When all was quiet, just as I was ready to fall asleep, my friend arrived looking for food. This time he was lucky. The mouse grabbed the food I left for him, and scuttled away.

Next day I did the same but this time placed the bread-crumbs closer to my hand. Every night I repeated the procedure, closer and closer, until he was eating out of my hand. It became obvious that the mouse realised that some humans were not so bad after all. He was running about the attic happily and was the source of much amusement for me.

When Mrs Grabovska said she felt sorry for me all alone in the attic, I told her about my friendship with the mouse. She laughed and said the neighbours had told her proudly how they had killed all the mice in the house.

Let me compare my situation with that of the mouse. That night, I waited for the mouse. Suddenly I heard a 'snap'. After that, my little friend did not appear again. I, on the other hand, survived.

★   ★   ★

I was almost killed several times during the Second World War. On this occasion, my family was staying in a Polish village, Grymbawoof, about thirty kilometres from Krakow. There were three or four Jewish families 'living' in Grymbawoof – like us kicked out of our hometown in Krakow by the Nazis. In the village there were two Polish policemen who co-operated with the Nazis.

The Nazis had taken all our possessions, including my piano

which I had enjoyed playing very much. Not having a piano anymore, I took up a smaller instrument, one that I was able to keep in the pocket of my trousers, a mouth organ.

I was known in the village as 'the musician' by the farmers who liked me because I could play the mouth organ quite well. I noticed that when they were drunk they became sentimental, and liked to sing. Not like some alcoholics who, after drinking, like to cry. The farmers there had a saying: 'It isn't the vodka that is strong, it is people who are weak.'

'Yoram, you bloody Jew, play for us!' they would demand after several glasses of 'bimber', the home-made vodka.

Just as I was getting used to the horror of this life in Grymbawoof, a new order came from above: 'All the villages around Krakow must be *Juden rein* – clean of Jews – by Tuesday, 6 a.m. No Jews are allowed to remain in the village.'

On that Tuesday, at 6 a.m., we were still packing the few things we had when the two Polish policemen entered. 'You, come with us!' they said to me, and they pushed me outside the house. I had only my trousers on, no shirt, and no shoes.

They took me to a field and I walked barefoot over the stubble without feeling any pain. Behind me were the two, half-drunk, policemen, carrying old and very long rifles. I heard the 'click click' of a gun being primed. I was not afraid. As a thirteen-year-old boy, I had nothing to lose. My only thoughts were for my poor mother.

One of the policemen said, 'Play for us before we kill you.' So I played a popular folk tune from the mountains, called *Pobili Sie Dwaj Gorale Ciupagami*, about two woodsmen fighting each other with axes. As far as I can remember, I played it without any emotion.

'Fine,' said the second policeman, 'and do you have any

vodka at home?' I answered, 'Sure, I have.' We always had vodka at home, because it was more valuable than money. 'So, run and bring the bottle,' I was told. 'But be quick, we have some more Jews to kill today.'

I ran home. There was no choice but to take them the vodka otherwise they would have killed my family. When I returned, they shared the bottle, and forgot all about me.

Happy ending.

Wartime

What can a little chap do,
For his Country, and for you?
What can a little chap do?

JOHN OXENHAM

'Oh, it'll be such fun,' their mother had said when she kissed
them goodbye at the station. 'Living in the country instead of
the stuffy old city. You'll love it, you see if you don't!' As if
Hitler had arranged this old war for their benefit, just so that
Carrie and Nick could be sent away in a train with gas masks
slung over their shoulder and their names on cards round their
necks. Labelled like parcels – Caroline Wendy Willow and
Nicholas Peter Willow – only with no address to be sent to.
None of them, not even the teachers, knew where they were
going.

NINA BAWDEN, *Carrie's War* (1973)

Most accounts of wartime evacuation concentrate on the
shocking arrival in middle-class homes of hordes of slum children from cities like London and Liverpool with head lice and
no table manners. Our experience, on the whole, was the
other way round.

NINA BAWDEN, *In My Own Time* (1994)

ROGER HANCOCK

Probably still hidden at the bottom of the deepest cellar in a country mansion in Somerset is a swastika hacked from the tailplane of a German fighter-bomber.

In the early Forties, my prep school was evacuated to a seven-thousand-acre estate at Hambridge in Somerset. The school lived in one wing of the mansion and the owners lived in the other.

One hot, sunny Sunday afternoon in the summer of 1944, my chum, Kirk, and I were standing above the ha-ha at the rear of the main building when we saw what looked like a German Heinkel losing height rapidly and apparently crash-landing in a field about two miles from the school. The plane didn't explode on impact probably because it had run out of fuel.

Keen to be the first at the scene of the accident, Kirk and I rushed to our bikes and pedalled like hell to the area where we saw the plane crash.

After about twenty minutes, we found the plane, which was on the ground in the corner of a field. Apart from a certain amount of oil spillage and minor damage to the nose, the plane was intact. The two-man crew was nowhere to be seen (are we surprised?!) so we got into the fuselage of the plane and proceeded to pull out some of the radio equipment as souvenirs.

We then hit on a brilliant wheeze (as it was called in the *Just William* era). Why not cut one of the swastikas off the tail and get it back to the school where we could hide it? We had a few tools in our saddlebags, including a small hacksaw, and after a while we managed very crudely to hack off the oil-covered swastika, which was about three-feet square.

Then we realised our main problem – how to get the jagged piece of metal back to the school? We decided the only way to achieve this would be to get on our bikes and hold the piece of metal between us as we cycled unsteadily back there.

As it was late on a Sunday afternoon, nobody was about when we finally made it back to the school grounds. We then remembered that, although totally out-of-bounds to the pupils, we had in fact illegally recced the deep cellars in the house a few months before.

The upshot was that we did manage to hide the tailplane swastika in one of the dusty, unused cellars and I'll be surprised if it's not still there today.

I only wish I'd retained the fearless (or stupid!) quality that I had on that summer afternoon nearly sixty years ago.

A meeting of the School Aircraft Spotters' Club

ROLF INHAUSER

My mother was told on Christmas Day, 1943, that my father had died. I was four years old. These two SS men in black leather coats with caps on their heads came to our house. I can see it clearly in my mind. I had on white gloves and I was smearing them green on the bark of a pear tree in the front garden. Later, the two men in black coats came out of the house and afterwards I saw my mother appear at a window. The memory fades there. According to my mother, when she told me my father had died, I replied: 'Oh, it doesn't matter. We will find another soldier.' I don't remember saying that. But I do remember going to the mountains with my father for the last time in August 1943. And I remember him leaving home. He had a huge, bluish-grey coloured wooden trunk with the head of a chamois, a mountain goat, painted on the lid.

My father died in Yugoslavia, in November 1943, fighting the partisans. He had been given a special order to capture Tito, perhaps because he came from the mountains and was a good climber and rider. Two of his SS officers accompanied him. The rest of the company were Italian special soldiers, and some *Ustachi* – Croats fighting on the German side. They went into a valley in the mountains of Yugoslavia where they came under machine gunfire from the partisans and they were all massacred.

My father was born in 1912. He was brought up in South

Tyrol, where he spoke Ladin, an old Romance dialect of the Inn valley. His father came from a well-off farming family but he had been disinherited. So my father had to make his own way in the world. First, he took an apprenticeship near the Austrian border, making farm machinery. After that, he couldn't find work because of the high unemployment. The only job that had any prospects was in the army. By chance, he joined the *Hundertschaft Roedel*, a company of one hundred soldiers under an officer called Roedel. It was this organisation that became the forerunner of the SS. My father was strong, big, and obviously quite clever. Very quickly, he climbed up the ladder. His rank in the SS was *Hauptscharführer*. He was a young man when he became Rudolf Hess's chief bodyguard and driver. I have a photograph of Hess inscribed by him to my father which is dated Christmas, 1935, when my father was twenty-three.

Christmas was a wonderful German family festival for children. But in our family it had no religious meaning. It was the same at Easter. There was an old Franconian custom of making a little Easter garden on wooden wheels, with grass made from moss or wood shavings, for the eggs. Some people in the villages put old wax figures in the garden, an Easter lamb, Christ as a child. But in my Easter garden I didn't have an Easter lamb or the yellow Catholic flag. My Easter garden, and the other Easter gardens of the kids around me, had a swastika flag.

I don't know where my father met my mother. They married in 1939, after I was born. She was twenty. I was born in Steinhöring, near Ebersberg, east of Munich. Steinhöring was the first of the *Lebensborn* maternity homes where they produced and bred the racially pure. It may have been that my mother went there for my birth because Steinhöring was famous for its maternity care and the privilege of the women-folk of high-ranking officers. I don't know. She was very beautiful with blue eyes and blond hair. My hair was white-blond as a small child. I went back to Steinhöring when I was about twenty and the building was still there. Around it, there was a concrete fence with Nazi emblems engraved on the bars. The *Hakenkreuz*, the swastika, had been knocked off them, but I did find one intact swastika hidden in some bushes behind the building.

I don't know what my father did after Hess flew to Britain in 1941 and was arrested. My mother gave me some official papers showing that in 1941 my father belonged to the *SS Standortkommandantur Dachau, Sonderkolonne*. The *Sonderkolonne* was a special unit at the garrison headquarters – the *Standortkommandantur*. I asked her, 'Why does it say Dachau?' And she replied immediately that he had nothing to do with the concentration camp and that the SS camps were grouped together by area and that Dachau was the area for the SS based around Munich.

Around this time we were living in Pullach, near Munich, in a house with a huge garden that joined the grounds of a castle. Our house was right opposite the quarters for Hitler's staff, the *Führerhauptquartier* called *Sonnwinkel*, which means Sunny Corner. Isn't that nice?

After the war it became, and still is, the West German military intelligence headquarters. Rudolf Hess and his family lived close by in Munchen Harlaching. I used to play with Hess's son, Wolf Rüdiger. My father bought an old wooden horse from a merry-go-round which he turned into a rocking horse. Once I pushed Wolf Rüdiger off the horse and his ear was squished under the rocker. Martin Bormann's family also lived in Pullach for a time. My mother told me that I didn't like one of the Bormann boys called Heinemann – an unusual first name – and that I had nicknamed him 'Heinemann Schweinemann'. Schweinemann means pig man.

The colour red is a strong memory. I remember the red leather seats of General Field Marshall Rommel's plane, a *Fieseler Storch*, in which I had a ride. The *Luftwaffe* used to land these small planes in a field used as pastureland for sheep not far from our house. The shepherd was my father's friend. I can remember sleeping with my father in the shepherd's cart as it was drawn by two donkeys, and the feeling of excitement and happiness.

I must have gone a few times to Hitler's retreat, Obersalzberg, in the mountains near Berchtesgaden, because my father would have accompanied Hess there. My mother told me on one occasion I had stomach ache and that when we arrived in Obersalzberg I vomited in Hitler's armoured car, the one that was sold in America in the Fifties. She said General Field Marshall Keitel, chief of the Wehrmacht, gave me an orange to make me feel better. It was my first orange.

When Munich was bombed, my mother and I moved to Nuremberg. Our house was bombed twice. I remember the crumbling walls, the sirens, and people screaming. The worst memory of my life is being in the air-raid shelter with my mother during the bombing. We were sitting on benches and a man next to me tried to hide under my legs. That was terrible because I was just a child.

Between about six and nine years old, I had the same dream night after night. Blood, just blood, and around the blood there was fine white sand. Nothing else, no voices, not me, nobody, just this blood and sand. I knew in this dream that when one grain of sand seeped into the blood everything was finished. And I would wake up screaming, and sweating.

Our playground was in the ruins of Nuremberg. We had no shoes. I still have something in my foot from playing barefoot. We collected shrapnel and ammunition and opened up cartridges. Many terrible things happened to children. A friend of mine lost an eye. There were horrible gang wars among children. I was a member of a gang from six to fifteen years old. We discovered the trains had to slow down for a bend in the track and the bigger boys would jump on the trains at this spot and take coal and food and we, the little ones, collected it in sacks.

Food had to be organised. During the war there was a chocolate that came in tin boxes called *Pilotenschokolade*, pilot's chocolate, which contained caffeine to keep the *Luftwaffe* awake. That was heaven. I can still taste it. After the war, I remember the first Coca-Cola, the first pineapple. The YMCA gave us sweets called lifesavers, and showed us *Mickey Mouse* films. For the older children there were re-education classes. At school, on Saturdays, we had a soup made from sweet potatoes provided by Quaker-*Speisung*, an American Quaker charity. My mother scolded me but I just could not eat this sweet potato soup in spite of my hunger. A happier memory is the tiny bar of Hershey chocolate the Quakers gave us on those Saturdays. It still exists in almost the same colour. I collected those Hershey bars and gave them to my mother for a Christmas present. It rankled me as an adolescent that I gave them to her and did not eat them myself!

I can still smell the American trucks. Gas had a different smell then. I remember black soldiers sitting in front of the schools, giving goodies to little children. These guys were kind, feeding hungry children with chocolate and so on. One of these black soldiers held out a goody for me when I was passing once with my mother. As I reached out for it, she pulled me away and said, 'Don't take it.' He said something to her. Years later, I remembered what it was. He said, 'SS Hure', which means SS whore.

I started school at six years old but there were very few teachers in Nuremberg after the war and the children ranged from beginners to sixteen-year-olds all in the same class. I felt fear and horror. Some of the older boys offered their sisters for money to American soldiers. I didn't understand, or only half understood, the graffiti in the toilets. I didn't do well at school because I could not concentrate. When I was thirteen, my mother sent me to a Catholic boarding school. The fees can't have cost much because as a widow, and social worker, she had very little money. I was expelled from this school and from several other similar boarding schools. In retrospect I realise that, although it was a horrible experience, it was at boarding school, away from my mother, that I learnt how to stand on my own two feet.

Life with my mother was awful. She would beat me, force me to kneel on logs until blood came, for some minor offence. She taught me to cook, to sew, to do the housework, and how to behave. It was a sort of brainwashing. She was always bothering me about personal hygiene. 'Wash your hands, be clean, in your mind and your body,' she would say. 'Be clean, clean, clean.' I stopped washing when I went to boarding school until one day I made my own mind up to start again.

My mother always talked of my father as a hero. There was a photograph of him on her table in his SS uniform with the badge of the skull on his cap. Day in and day out she poured the sadness she felt for the loss of her husband over me until I felt I was suffocating. When I was seven or so, I suddenly realised that other children had uncles, grandmothers, and grandfathers, and I asked my mother, 'Where is my family?' All she said was, 'Oh, they died a long time ago.'

Years later an uncle of mine, my father's brother who was the only one to survive of twelve children, made contact with me. He had been some high officer in the *Luftwaffe*, and a journalist in the war. When I was fifteen or so this uncle told me that my mother was Jewish. When he said that, my mind froze in shock.

At the time, I didn't want to discuss what he had told me with my mother. I did not know who else I could talk to about it, and I felt alone. It was years later when I did try to talk to her about it but she refused to answer my questions. She has never admitted being a Jew to me. My father must have known she was Jewish because my uncle told me their marriage was one of the so-called privileged mixed-race marriages which were allowed in certain cases.

My mother is still pro-Nazi. After the war, she kept in contact with Frau Hess. The letters used to arrive in sealed envelopes bound with the censor's blue, red and white striped tape. I once asked my mother the meaning of this unusual tape, and she replied, 'Oh they are just letters from Frau Hess.' Although she has always denied being Jewish, I do remember now her telling me once that she and her brother had wanted to emigrate to some South American country, and I asked her, 'So why didn't you go?' And her reply was, 'Why are you asking me that? It was forbidden to leave.'

When I was eighteen, and still at boarding school, my mother gave me the money for a driving licence. I wondered why because it cost a fortune, and we didn't have a car. But when the summer vacation came, the reason became clear. She wanted me to drive her to Yugoslavia to see the valley where my father had died. This trip was sheer horror. We drove in a white Volkswagen, like a marriage coach. The one good memory is meeting a guy about my age who, as a child, had carried information from one partisan group to another. He showed me two bullet wounds in his chest that he had caught in the crossfire between the lines. While we were there my mother scattered handfuls of forget-me-not seeds on the ground which she had brought from Germany. I could have killed her.

A few years ago, she told me a story. Some time in the Seventies, she found out from two old school friends that her paediatrician from her childhood in Nuremberg was living in Haifa and trying to make contact with her again. She had liked my mother very much. So my mother wrote to her and this Doctor Steckelmacher sent her a ticket for Haifa. When she arrived, Doctor Steckelmacher's son told her that his mother was dying in hospital but that she had said to him, 'If Ida Eckstein comes, I would like to see her.' My mother replied, 'No, I don't want to see her. I want to remember her as she was.' The next day she returned home. That was the last time I tried to talk to my mother about her being Jewish. I said to her, 'Don't you want to tell me about your family?' And she said, 'It's better that you don't know.' A friend of mine is looking in Israel for Doctor Steckelmacher's son. I would like to meet him.

When I went to the United States for the first time, some Jews recognised me as Jewish. That was strange. It's not the looks. I have mixed feelings about wanting to know more about my past. Sometimes yes, sometimes no. Do I feel Jewish? What's Jewish? I don't know who I am – but then, who does?

TOM MASCHLER

One of my first memories is of Berlin. I recall a loud knock on our front door and outside stood two Nazi officers. They had come for my father. But by good fortune he was away at the time and so they confiscated our house instead. It was that simple. My mother was told to pack an overnight bag and then to give up the keys to our house. I was invited to choose a single object from my father's study, something I would be allowed to take away with me. My father had built up a collection of manuscripts and letters, including an especially valuable manuscript by Thomas Mann and another by Herman Hesse. He also possessed letters by famous artists, among them Van Gogh and Cezanne. Oblivious of the value of these treasures I chose a large crayon – red at one end and blue at the other. I was five years old and my choice was characteristic of that of any small child. My mother prepared a little rucksack for me and I tucked the crayon into it. Shortly we were ready to leave our home to the officers. In retrospect, I am surprised at how polite they had been. My mother was naturally distraught but I walked down the street quite cheerfully with her.

We went on foot to visit some friends who lived nearby. Our plan was to get to Sweden and from there to catch a boat to the United States, where we had many relatives. It was 1938 and communications were still functioning. As it turned out, we missed the last boat bound for the States from Sweden and we caught a ship to England instead. There we could stay with my mother's brother, Alfons, who was a doctor in Harrow, a London suburb. We stayed with my uncle and aunt for several months. They were always kind and we shared the family life with their two daughters both of my age. I could not help feeling that they viewed having taken us under their roof as an act of charity and it made me uncomfortable.

Then the air raids began and every day we learned of more destruction from German bombers. Especially in London. The word 'evacuation' was on everyone's lips. The concern was especially to arrange for children to go to the countryside as far away from the bombs as possible. My mother was eager to attempt to make her own arrangements rather than to join one of the official groups. She was able to read English and so she began to look through advertisements in newspapers. This is how she found the De Salis family. They required a 'lady cook' for their residence, Holly Cross House. It was situated in Berkshire some four miles from Henley and three from Wargrave. My mother was offered the job. Shortly thereafter we were installed in a cottage which was known as 'The Coachman's House' and had been inhabited by a coachman who drove a horse and cart in days gone by. Lady De Salis, the mistress of the Holly Cross House, was a tyrant. She suffered from acute arthritis, and could be heard clattering along the tiles with her two sticks as she made her way each morning to the kitchen. She seemed to delight in tormenting my mother, who had never worked for anyone before. We were rather well off in Germany.

I was sent to the local school. This was in Wargrave and was called the Robert Piggott Junior School. It was neither better nor worse than the average village school. The school still stands and I visited it recently, some sixty years later. At Holly Cross House my school was referred to as 'the street kids' school'.

It will come as no great surprise to learn that I was not allowed to play with the grandchildren of the house. I avenged myself by stealing from time to time a precious nectarine from the greenhouse. More daringly, I also stole some wooden lifeboats which were resting along the deck of a massive galleon that stood proudly in the hallway of the main house. Initially there were two rows of lifeboats, one each side of the masts. I stole a pair of them from one end. I then stole two more from the other end to even things up, so to speak, and the same again a further two from each end. By this time the lifeboat showing was a bit thin. For safety, I took the rest of the boats, being a further eight.

We had virtually no money and even the bus fare to school was out of reach. Consequently, I walked three miles each way daily. In spring, I enjoyed my walk especially as I got to know the birds in the hedges and delighted in the nests and their magnificent eggs. Then I would look out daily as the eggs began to hatch and finally I was overjoyed by the birth of the babies. Another great pleasure was to get to know the people who lived along the country road. The sight of a six-year-old passing by on foot twice a day fascinated them and I was frequently invited in for a drink and a bun.

At school I was an average pupil. The only thing at which I excelled was organising a small gang of five children. We were for hire all year round but the most memorable time was when it came to the apple harvest. We indulged in an activity called 'scrumping' which involved robbing orchards. Two or three lookouts took up position in strategic places and the

others would frantically pick the fruit. It was exciting and it was also mildly dangerous. In addition, it was rather profitable. I would take my share of the money home to my mother and I felt like the breadwinner of the family whilst my father was in London acting as an unpaid air-raid warden.

Life continued on much the same lines for five years except that conditions in the De Salis household got worse and worse as the war progressed. Initially my mother worked alongside a butler, two pantry maids, two cleaners and a chauffeur. Finally, as the staff left to join the war she was expected to undertake all duties. At this time white dustsheets were laid out to cover the furniture in most rooms. Much as I disliked the family, it was a sad spectacle.

After five years at the Robert Piggott Junior School, I received a grant to go to Leighton Park, a Quaker boarding school and a minor public school at Reading, some forty miles from Wargrave. Unfortunately, the grant did not stretch to my being a full-time boarder and so for the first two years I was lodged with six different families. Being a displaced person seemed my fate.

Before I went to Leighton Park there was an interlude in France. My mother had decided that I should learn French 'properly' and that meant learning the language in France. In order to achieve this successfully she wanted me to spend a summer with French people who spoke no English. Now that I was just twelve years old seemed the right moment to her. Since my mother did not know of an appropriate family she determined to find one. Her method was to take me to Brittany, where she chose a fishing village called Roscoff on the north coast.

No sooner had we arrived, she took off down the high

street and began to knock upon the front door of whichever house she thought looked promising. Her proposition was simply that the family should offer me board and lodging for which they would be paid at cost and I should remain with them for two months. There seemed to be precious little in it from the French family's point of view and that is no doubt the reason a dozen households turned us down. I was growing increasingly embarrassed but then, at what looked like the grandest house of all, we struck lucky. It was a bonus that the house happened to belong to the Mayor of Roscoff and he had three sons and a very pretty daughter.

During my stay I never received so much as a single phone call from my mother, and just two letters. This was part of her method no doubt. The second of the letters dealt entirely with the arrangements to be made for my return. Whilst she had regarded her presence as important to the outward journey, it seemed superfluous for the way back. Aged twelve, she reckoned there was no reason why I should not find my own way to England. Of course, she turned out to be quite right. She was also right to suppose that I would become reasonably fluent in French. A week after my return, term began at Leighton Park.

My new school was an admirable place, and I could write at length about my years there, but I prefer to restrict myself to just one episode that was for me a highlight. The school had a greatly respected institution known as the Travel Scholarship. Entrants were called upon to write an account of a journey they hoped to undertake. I chose a journey to Israel. Being a Jewish refugee, I naturally wanted to become familiar with the land and I especially wanted to work in several Kibbutzim. They were a concept that had caught my imagination early on.

Well, I won the Travel Scholarship, which was for the sum of fifty pounds, but it was a condition that this sum should be sufficient to pay for everything involved. And so in my case winning could only be 'conditional'. I shall never forget my anger when the Headmaster announced in front of the whole school that the Travel Scholarship had been won by me subject to 'practicability'. I had written in my application that I would hitchhike to Marseille and there I would get a job on an Israeli steamer, earning my passage by washing dishes. I had read of such things and did not anticipate any obstacle. The fact that I was fifteen seemed to me irrelevant. Given my Headmaster's scepticism I was doubly determined to prove my point.

It occurred to me that I could write to the Israeli Prime Minister, Ben Gurion, explaining my predicament. I did so and to my enormous delight he wrote back saying that he had passed my letter on to the Ministry of Transport and Communication and, two weeks later, I received a letter from them telling me to present myself at the offices of a certain shipping company in Marseille on a particular day at the beginning of July. Washing dishes was certainly my task. Two to three thousand a day. This was my first independent journey and gave me a taste for travelling which has become an important part of my life.

BILL DE QUICK

I was born on 10 June 1945, in Plymouth. My mother, who was married, had a wartime love affair with a coloured American soldier while he was stationed in Devon. Before her husband returned from the war, my mother applied to a Church of England institution called The Waifs & Strays Society – I think the boys were the waifs and the girls the strays. It's called the Children's Society now. I was accepted into their care and, when I was five months old, sent to a nursery in Wiltshire.

My mother took me on the train from Callington to Bere Alston to catch the connection to Salisbury. When she got to Bere Alston there was another woman in the same situation and the two of them travelled on to Salisbury together. They were met at Salisbury station by the Matron and the Sister of the nursery. The parting was traumatic and heartbreaking and as I was put into a car outside the station, my mother noticed some soldiers who were going by had stopped and fallen quiet as they watched the scene. Then they went back home on the train. It was 1st November 1945.

Clouds was a huge house bought by the Children's Society for their nursery. My earliest memories are all of Clouds. The first is of a large bedroom and looking out of the window on to rolling downland, lovely trees, a sort of Capability Brown landscape, and seeing a fox cross the park. The dormitories were named after flowers – Tulip, Daffodil and Primrose. We each had a nurse who looked after us the whole time we were there to give us a continuity of care. That was very forward thinking. I still visit some of the nurses who remember me. They were only youngsters at the time, sixteen- to eighteen-year-old trainee nurses.

We used to go on lovely walks on to a ridge and look down into a valley and up the other side. The bluebells seemed enormous, I suppose because I was little. David called it his paradise. David and I were like brothers, about the same colour. Our beds were together in the dormitory and he is the first person I can remember.

We left Clouds together when we were six years old and were sent to a 'home', a boys' institution in Burgess Hill, Sussex. After eighteen months, David was sent away to another home. I don't know why. It was devastating, and I only saw him again briefly when I was about ten at one of the big Children's Society parties.

The home at St Luke's, Burgess Hill, was very different from Clouds. It was a big house with dormitories numbered 1, 2, 3 and 4. The boys were aged five or six up to school-leaving age of fifteen. I had never come across rough people before, older boys who would hit and threaten you.

I can remember walking into the playroom on the first day and the Master saying, 'Here's a boy who has come to join us.' Then he left, and this little boy said, 'Would you like to play with my car?' And I got down on my hands and knees on the lino and we pushed this toy car to each other. Richard Severn. Same age as me. He remained my friend until we left.

Some boys had parents or mothers who would visit them but even then I was not curious about my own background. If I was asked, I said my parents were dead, and if I was asked where I was born, I hadn't the faintest, so I said London. Perhaps I did not think about them because we had 'uncles' and 'aunts' who befriended us. They would come down once a month or so and take us out to Brighton and places. Mine were a lovely couple from Shepherds Bush, Mr and Mrs Evans. Once we went to their home. They were a great support. And I had another 'aunt', Miss Filmer, who lived nearby in Ditchling in a house with an apple orchard. Every September I would go there for a week and, between times, she would take me out. We went all round Sussex in her Morris Minor car, once as far as Arundel. I remember going to Chichester, and the Lewes area, and little tea places in Haywards Heath. She also taught me manners, how to hold a knife and fork, to say please and thank you, and to pass round the butter, all those little things. I continued to see her long after I left the home until she died, an old lady in her eighties.

Others did their part for the children. Two brothers, called Box, from Haywards Heath had a projector and they came perhaps twice a year to show us old cartoons of *Tom and Jerry* and loads of Charlie Chaplin films. Sometimes we would go to their house for a tea party. And Martin Buckmaster, who became a viscount, took a group of us to London Zoo and other places. I remember he turned up once in Arab robes to show us how a sheikh would dress. It was most impressive.

It was only when I was about twelve that I started to wonder about my parents. One day I was at the pianola. No one else was in the room. I just stopped playing and started to feel sorry for myself. The Matron, Mrs Gray, came in and wanted to know why I was upset, and when I asked her about my parents she said, 'They are dead.' And then the Master, Mr Gray, came in and said, 'Oh, you will be all right. Come on, off you go.' That was that! He was a tall chap, Australian, always whistling. If you did anything wrong, he would clip you round the ear. Certain boys were always picked on. Matron would tell him of some misdemeanour and he would say, 'Right, up to bed.' Then he stood by the door and as the boy went past he would clout him round the head. Some of the lads, the regulars, knew to dive down. I was sent up to bed once because I refused to eat my caraway seed cake. To this day, I can't eat it.

Although they were strict, the Grays did look after us in an odd sort of way. At Christmas, they gave us a good time and always took us to a pantomime. There was a ladder at the end of a corridor and we used to climb up to a box at the top to post our letters to Santa. These would then be passed on to the 'uncles' and 'aunts'. We had a Santa's Grotto in the large dining room. It never occurred to me that Santa wasn't someone dressed up. Santa gave you a little present. And then there were the presents from your 'uncles' and 'aunts'. I had a cricket set one Christmas from the Evanses.

It wasn't a bad institution as such, although there was no affection from the Grays. Yet, compared with children in inner-city homes, we did quite well there. We walked just over a mile to the local primary school. The secondary modern school was brand new. Everyone there knew we were from St Luke's and called us Lukeys. I was the only coloured person there in a school of seven hundred and fifty but it was never an issue. I did not see myself as different, although one occasion does come to mind. I liked singing and was in the school music society. We were going to perform 'The King of Sherwood', and all the boys had to put chocolate stuff on their legs because we didn't have leggings. And I thought, I don't need to do that.

There was no homework for the St Luke's boys. Just as well, because there was nowhere to sit down at a desk or table to do your homework. We all shared the playroom, which had a huge covered billiard table down the middle. Down each side of the room there was a long undivided box with several lids along the top. The lid lifted by a hole and underneath was a section for your belongings. There were shelves of books in the room with classic stories like *Treasure Island,* which kind people had given to the home. No one read to us. I liked reading. We had *Rupert* annuals and some *Giles.* The *Just William* stories. It never crossed my mind that it would have been nice to have William's home life. My life was in St Luke's.

Every Saturday we were allotted a job for the week, it could be washing up, peeling the potatoes, putting out the cutlery in the dining room, weeding the yard, polishing the lino floors with a buffer. We did all the cleaning. Eventually they got a potato-peeling machine, which I thought was awful. I did a much better job than the machine which left all the eyes in. I remember toast and dripping – that was good – and the huge pots of porridge on the Aga.

On Sundays we went to church twice, morning service and Sunday school. If you were in the choir, you went to evensong as well. I had a good voice but was never in the choir. Talking about this the other day, I was told it was probably because I was coloured. I hadn't thought of that. It was odd because I did have one of the best voices in the home, and quite a few of the boys were in the choir. I didn't mind so much because it would have meant going to church three times on Sundays. St John's was very high church. I loved the services and the ritual, and still do.

The church was opposite the home and on St George's Day

the scouts would use our yard to line up before parading into the church for the service which we did not attend. The Grays did not allow us to join the Boy Scouts or any other local organisations. One of the highlights of the year, though, was going on a scout camping holiday for two weeks. It was usually for those of us who didn't have parents. A chap from the Children's Society head office would meet us at a railway station near the camp – one year it was near Wimborne in Dorset – and drive us in a Land Rover to the campsite. We met boys from other homes who were in the scouts. That was great fun. So we did manage to get out quite a bit.

It was work on Saturday mornings but the afternoons were free. There was a cinema at the end of the garden and on Saturdays five boys from the home were given free tickets, but we had to be back by five o'clock. This meant you could see the B film but not the end of the feature film, or the other way round. There was no way you could be late back.

The first film I remember seeing was *Where No Vultures Fly*, which I thought was brilliant. But when I saw it to the end on television some years ago, it was a great disappointment. Another film I remember seeing was *Johnny on the Run*. I did see that one to the end but it must have been touch and go to get back in time.

In our free time, I liked to play cricket in the garden. There was a large wooden hut in the garden, known as the den. It had a huge mat where some boys had boxing and wrestling contests. At the other end of the room, there were bars and ropes, like a gym, and a little window. A very useful little window. When the Grays had their day off, Thursday, they always went to Brighton for a Chinese meal. From this little window we could watch them going down the road, and once they were past the war memorial we knew they were on their way. The Master would invariably forget something and come back, so we used to give them about ten minutes before we went on the rampage. There was an old wind-up gramophone and hundreds of records. I remember the 'Laughing Policeman' and how the needle went up and down and round on the thin floppy record. We also had a tennis table and, after the Grays retired, formed a team called the Pentagon and beat the local teams.

I must have been fourteen – the Grays had left, which was probably just as well – when I discovered that I was not an orphan. A group of us had been handed our record cards and sent to the clinic up the road for an inoculation. I was sitting down waiting my turn, very quiet, when I looked at this card and saw a strange address in Devon. I thought to myself, Who do I know in Devon? I had to think where Devon was! So I memorised the address as best I could before I handed in the card to the clinic. A few months later, at Christmas-time, I sent a card to the address. I didn't know who to address the card to, so I put 'To Sir or Madam'. We were told at school that was what you had to write when you did not know the name. So that's what I did, wishing whoever it was a Happy Christmas, and sent the card off. Then after Christmas, I received a letter. It was from my mother.

My mother wrote that she was always thinking of me but had not made contact with me because of her husband. She hoped I would do well in my life, and added that my father's name was Brown. I still have the letter.

There was no more contact. It wasn't until years later, after I had moved to London, that I showed the letter to my friend Tom and he wrote a careful letter to my mother suggesting we

HR. TAVISTOCK,
DEVON.

30.12.59.

Dear Billy,

I was so thrilled to receive your X mas card, it is very pretty, it seems so strange to hear from you for the very first time. I have often thought about you, wished you were making out allright. I only wanted to keep in touch. But as my husband did not want _____ had to make my life with him, there was _____ thing else I could do.

I would love to see you, but it would never do, as it would only bring heartbreak & I had enough of that the day I had to part with you.

I have a boy just a year younger than you, & a boy of _____ one of five. I have a daughter O live who is seventeen, & she was just three when you _____ born, during the war.

We are expecting another child in

March. I hope you have been fairly happy in life, it is supposed to be one of the best homes in England, so I hope you have been allright, & I shall allways pray for you, so you will know there is someone watching over you.

I hope & pray that you will make your way in the world allright, & that one day in the future you will meet someone you will like, & will be able to settle down in a home of your own home.

I am sending something which might enamble you to get something you will like. I wish it could be more, but I will not forget your birthday June 10th. I will close now for the time, with my sincere best wishes

From your friend,
Eileen Warwick. x x x x v x

P.S. I gave you my name, but your fathers name is really Brown.

P.P.S. I will have your photo when you were a _____ a lovly baby you was too. x x x meet. She agreed, and we arranged to meet on a Saturday in June 1970 underneath Drake's statue on Plymouth Hoe.

So Tom and I went to Plymouth by train and got on to the Hoe nice and early, and every time a single woman went by we would think, Is that her? No. Is it that one? No. And then Tom said, 'Here she comes.' He was right. He recognised her in me or vice versa. Then Tom left us and my mother and I had a meal in a hotel. She showed me photographs of her children. I had some photographs too. And we hit it off straight away. We knew we were going to be great friends, and always have been.

I call her Eileen – not mother. Other people I have talked to in my situation said the same. When I talked to my mother about it she said, 'You can call me Eileen.' And my father? That's another story.

ONORA O'NEILL

In 1948 I was six years old, and my father was posted to Frankfurt to head British Liaison with the American Control Commission which governed a quarter of Germany during the post-war years. As a wartime child I had been used to frequent moves, but had never been abroad. Although we were not by then an army family, we were to travel by train and ferry with army families going out for a stint in occupied Germany.

At grimy Liverpool Street station we joined interminable queues, took an even more grimy train to Harwich and then walked up a memorably steep gangplank to board the ferry for the Continent. I stood proudly in all the queues, holding my small cardboard suitcase containing assorted toys.

The next morning we disembarked at the oddly named Hook of Holland, and once again waited for an age, this time in a large waiting room. There were more mothers and children than I had ever seen. Suddenly the crowd stirred. Some people climbed on to chairs and tables; some screamed. Then a rat appeared, moving rather slowly among the crowd and – as I realised only in retrospect – causing this unusual behaviour by grown-ups. As a well-brought-up country child I knew what to do: I raised my little suitcase, banged it on the rat and (rather against the odds) killed it.

This was not the expected move. To my consternation I found myself being scolded by a strange man in uniform. My mother intervened, and the scolding ended. The rat was dead, I was in tears, and I have still not forgotten my first experience on the continent of Europe.

Christmas

'Christmas won't be Christmas without any presents,' grumbled Jo, lying on the rug.

LOUISA M. ALCOTT, *Little Women* (1868–9)

'Get back to the Presents.'

'There were the Useful Presents: engulfing mufflers of the old coach days, and mittens made for giant sloths; zebra scarfs of a substance like silky gum that could be tug-o'-warred down to the galoshes; blinding tam-o'-shanters like patchwork tea cosies and bunny-suited busbies and balaclavas for victims of head-shrinking tribes; from aunts who always wore wool next to the skin there were moustached and rasping vests that made you wonder why the aunts had any skin left at all; and once I had a little crocheted nose bag from an aunt now, alas, no longer whinnying with us. And pictureless books in which small boys, though warned with quotations not to, *would* skate on Farmer Giles' pond and did and drowned; and books that told me everything about the wasp, except why.'

'Go on to the Useless Presents.'

'Bags of moist and many-coloured jelly babies and a folded flag and a false nose and a tram-conductor's cap and a machine that punched tickets and rang a bell; never a catapult; once, by mistake that no one could explain, a little hatchet; and a celluloid duck that made, when you pressed it, a most unducklike sound, a mewing moo that an ambitious cat might make who wished to be a cow; and a painting book in which I could make the grass, the sea and the animals any colour I pleased, and still the dazzling sky-blue sheep are grazing in the red field under the rainbow-billed and pea-green birds.

'Hardboileds, toffee, fudge and allsorts, crunches, cracknels, humbugs, glaciers, marzipan, and butterwelsh for the Welsh. And troops of bright tin soldiers who, if they could not fight, could always run. And Snakes-and-Families and Happy Ladders. And Easy Hobbi-Games for Little Engineers, complete with instructions.

'Oh, easy for Leonardo! And a whistle to wake up the old man next door to make him beat on the wall with his stick to shake our pictures off the wall.

'And a packet of cigarettes; you put one in your mouth and stood at the corner of the street and you waited for hours, in vain, for an old lady to scold you for smoking a cigarette, and then with a smirk you ate it. And then it was breakfast under the balloons.'

DYLAN THOMAS, *A Child's Christmas in Wales* (1978)

When the children have been good,
That is, be it understood,
Good at meal times, good at play,
Good all night and good all day,
They shall have the pretty things
Merry Christmas always brings.

DR HEINRICH HOFFMAN, *Struwwelpeter* (1848)

Christmas was good wherever it was. How long the grey Edinburgh light took to seep through until one could see the shape of one's stocking at the foot of the bed. Was it as big as last time? Bigger? That promising bulge? Boy and I had separately helped to fill one another's stockings but had kept firm secrets. Some of the presents were wrapped, anyhow. I can't think I ever believed in Father Christmas coming down the chimney, but I gave the notion lip service to please my elders as my own children have kindly done for me.

NAOMI MITCHISON, *Small Talk* (1973)

Winter

That winter was freezing cold with about a foot of snow. I loved it, but Mum had always been paranoiacally afraid of falling down on ice. My father or I had to get all the shopping in. The only time she ventured out in the snow was a trip to the end of the garden to castrate my snowman. I had made a wonderful six-foot high one. I reached the top of it by standing on a little step or two of snow I'd made at its foot. I gave him cinders for eyes and a dirty grin. About halfway down I smeared more cinders for pubic hair and pinched one of Mum's carrots for a penis. Mum's sense of bourgeois propriety proved even greater than the snow-phobia and she trudged down the garden to emasculate my creation. Neither my father nor I would oblige. It was his kind of joke.

FIONA PITT-KETHLEY, *My Schooling* (2000)

All shod with steel,
We hissed along the polished ice in games
Confederate, imitative of the chase
And woodland pleasures, – the resounding horn,
The pack loud bellowing, and the hunted hare.
So through the darkness and the cold we flew,
And not a voice was idle; with the din,
Meanwhile, the precipices rang aloud;
The leafless trees and every icy crag
Tinkled like iron; while the distant hills
Into the tumult sent an alien sound
Of melancholy not unnoticed, while the stars
Eastward were sparkling clear, and in the west
The orange sky of evening died away.
Not seldom from the uproar I retired
Into a silent bay, or sportively
Glanced sideway, leaving the tumultuous throng,
To cut across the image of a star
That gleamed upon the ice; and oftentimes,
When we had given our bodies to the wind,
And all the shadowy banks on either side
Came sweeping through the darkness, spinning still
The rapid line of motion, then at once
Have I, reclining back upon my heels,
Stopped short; yet still the solitary cliffs
Wheeled by me – even as if the earth had rolled
With visible motion her diurnal round!
Behind me did they stretch in solemn train,
Feebler and feebler, and I stood and watched
Till all was tranquil as a dreamless sleep.

WILLIAM WORDSWORTH, from *The Prelude*, Bk 1, (1805–06)

Tuesday, 12 January 1875

John Hatherell told me this evening that he recollects when a boy being one of the bearers at the burial of a gypsy girl 12 years of age. He had forgotten her name but we looked in the parish registers and found the entry of the funeral. The girl's name was 'Limpedy Buckland'. She was buried in Langley Burrell Churchyard in the year 1809 on the 29th of April. She died in the tents of her people in Sutton Lane opposite the gate of Sand Furlong. The road was then a green lane. When John and the other lads who were to be bearers reached the tents of the tribe they found a clean white cloth laid upon the green grass with bread, cheese and beer, and an old woman, the mother or grandmother of the dead girl, put her hand into her pocket and gave each of the bearer lads a shilling.

Easter Sunday, 16 April 1876

John Hatherell, the good old sawyer, now sleeps in the same God's acre to which he helped carry the gipsy girl Limpedy Buckland to her burial more than sixty years ago.

REVD. FRANCIS KILVERT, *Kilvert's Diary* (1944)

TIM PIGOTT-SMITH

When I was a child, my father got a job working for the *East African Standard*, the main newspaper in Kenya. We lived in Nairobi for a couple of years and stayed in a bungalow. We had a cook and a houseboy. People did then. We made trips to the national game reserves; I have one image in my mind of young lion cubs at play. I don't think this memory was photograph-induced, but I can't be certain.

In Nairobi, I developed an abscess in my ear and was prescribed what was then the equivalent of penicillin – M & B drugs. M & B stood for May and Bryant, the name of the manufacturing company. The drugs didn't work. More were prescribed. They didn't work. I became sicker and sicker, and it was decided that my mother should bring me home. Dad had to serve out his contract. I was four.

On the boat home I was still being prescribed M & B. In photographs, I appear pretty ghastly – pale and drugged – and my mum looks very stressed. I went into a coma. A request was put out on board ship for a doctor to come and look at a sick child. They thought I was dying. A doctor turned up. He examined me, and asked for my case history. He just said, 'Stop the drugs.' I came out of the coma. M & B drugs contained sulphur to which, it was later discovered, I was allergic. They were slowly killing me. By the time I had gone into what would have been a final coma, my blood was ninety-six per cent white – the sulphur had destroyed nearly all my red blood corpuscles.

I have a memory of waking up on the ship and, finding myself alone, I wandered round the corridors looking for signs of life. The memory is very personal – the camera is subjective – I don't see me, I see the bed, and the corridors of the ship. I remember getting out of bed and sliding to the ground tentatively, as if testing its reality. I felt my way out of the room and into the brighter corridor. I don't remember doors. I had a sense of excitement – a feeling that I was off to explore. I have no memory of finding anyone, or of how I got back. I do remember very clearly a sense of well-being, of feeling light-headed. Did this occur when I awoke from the coma? Surely, there would have been people with me. The experience has always felt to me the way people describe 'out-of-body experiences', and I sometimes think it might have been a dream or hallucination rather than an actual event.

Over twenty years later, I was appearing in a theatre in Rome and I was able to visit the doctor who stopped the drugs. My mother had kept in touch with him – not surprisingly, she felt a huge debt of gratitude. His name was Dr Leonard Hirsch, and he was a German Jew. Retired now, he lived with his sister on a hill overlooking the Eternal City. We had tea. He sweetly resisted any enquiries on my part into his background from which, I have always surmised, that it was pretty awful – not teatime chat. He was a charming man, quiet gentle, hospitable and generous. It was wonderful to meet him. To thank him. He modestly shrugged away the notion that he had saved my life.

Sundays

On Sunday as I walked in the garden I happened to take the cat in my arms. My father saw me and seriously reproved my levity, remarking that on the Lord's Day he was ashamed to observe me demeaning myself with so much profaneness.

WILLIAM GODWIN, Autobiographical fragment (1800)

I used to go to Sunday School at 10 o'clock, followed by Morning Service at eleven, followed by Afternoon Sunday School at 2.30, followed by Evening Service at 6 o'clock. And this was my natural Sunday life . . . It certainly was quite a rigorous routine. I think perhaps it was a bit too much. When you have been four times on Sundays, you do tend to react against it rather sharply. I can remember asking if I could go out for a walk with a friend on Sunday evening and that wasn't allowed.

MARGARET THATCHER, *Maggie: The First Lady*, ITV1 (6 March 2003)

The memory of seaside Sundays is strong and brilliant too. Here again, even on holiday, the hand of Methodism still took its stern grip on us. Even to set foot on the beach on the Sabbath Day was forbidden. Buckets and spades and balls and bathing drawers were put away as if they were devices of the devil. Others might trip down the steps of horse-drawn bathing cabins to disport themselves in the Sunday sea, but not us. Donkey rides, games, running, ice-creams, pop: all were taboo.

H. E. BATES, *The Vanished World* (1969)

Nothing is more difficult than to determine what a child takes in, and does not take in, of its environment and its teaching. This fact is brought home to me by the hymns which I learned as a child, and never forgot. They mean to me almost more than the finest poetry, and they have for me a more permanent value, somehow or other ...

Each gentle dove
And sighing bough
That makes the eve
So fair to me
Has something far
Diviner now
To draw me back
To Galilee.
O Galilee, sweet Galilee
Where Jesus loved so much to be,
O Galilee, sweet Galilee,
Come sing thy songs again to me!

To me the word Galilee has a wonderful sound. The Lake of Galilee! I don't want to know where it is. I never want to go to Palestine. Galilee is one of those lovely, glamorous worlds, not places, that exist in the golden haze of a child's half-formed imagination.

D. H. LAWRENCE, 'Hymns in a Man's Life', *Phoenix II* (1968)

As a child – aged four, five, six or seven – it is natural to see the landscape one reads about. So I thought of the big ponds near the pit where Dad worked as Galilee. The Valley of the Shadow of Death was a lane descending between overhanging hedges where you tended to want to whistle – but I was a timid child anyway and the Forest itself was a labyrinth of old oaks and beeches and ash trees. The words of both of those hymns and the Bible, and fairy stories, too, fitted very happily into that landscape.

DENNIS POTTER, 'Desert Island Discs', BBC Radio 4 (1977)

Wrong was showing-off, being disobedient, being rude, telling stories, doing weekday things – or thinking weekday thoughts on Sundays. I had done so much wrong I knew I must end in Hell and, what was worse, I could imagine it. Sometimes when Miss Craig had jerked me and thumped me into bed she would look at me grimly and say: 'Aye, you're here now but you don't know where you'll be when you wake up.'

LOUIS MACNEICE, *The Strings Are False* (1965)

At the age of seven we were allowed to attend the magnificent midnight mass at Easter. I remember one solemn service in particular, the priest coming out to administer Holy Communion to the children, and my brother and I, dressed in white piqué with red ties under our stiff white collars, being brought up to him. Behind us there was an orderly row of schoolboys in tight-fitting blue uniforms with silver buttons, and among them must have been the model pupil Vladimir Ulyanov (Lenin). I remember too an occasion when I stopped, deeply struck, before an image of the resurrected Christ which was so illuminated as to appear transparent and seemed to me to be alive. As a boy, Vladimir Ulyanov must have also looked at that image and, perhaps, laughed heartily to himself while keeping up a devout appearance – if we are to believe his own story that he threw his baptismal cross into the dustbin at about the age of fourteen. There was no duplicity, however, about my own feelings, and in a childish way I was deeply religious.

ALEXANDER KERENSKY, *The Kerensky Memoirs* (1966)

Our usual bedtime was six-thirty (we were six and four years old, put to bed at the same time for Nanny's convenience). The service began just when we were normally being tucked in, but we would be there! We were going to be out in the darkness of night, under the huge red harvest moon, and then in the brilliant church, and then, when we got home, we were going to have not ordinary bedtime milk and biscuits, but *real supper*!

And the church truly *was* brilliant. As soon as we were through the door, there was the font under its rich wild wreath, surrounded by pyramids of fruit and vegetables with a vast and glorious golden pumpkin as the centre-piece. All the ends of the pews, the whole way up the aisle, had sheaves of wheat and oats and barley tied to them. The screen and the pulpit were lavishly decorated with dahlias, michaelmas daisies and chrysanthemums mixed with more wheat, oats and barley, and in each window's wide recess a different still-life had been composed, some of them including loaves of bread and baskets of eggs (custom dictated who decorated which window and they vied with each other to splendid effect). It would have been gorgeous enough in daylight, and in the glow of lamp and candlelight it was magical. *And* – for us this was an enchanting finishing touch – there were bats flittering about up near the roof; *and* the hymns were the best we had ever heard. We were so much taken with one of them that we went on chanting it for days afterwards.

We plough the fields and sca-tter
The good seed on the land
But it is fed and wa-a-tered
By God's almighty hand . . .

I still sometimes sing that hymn when I'm driving safely out of the hearing of anyone with a good ear.

DIANA ATHILL, *Yesterday Morning* (2002)

Samad looked at his clipboard, underlined something in pen three times and turned to the parent-governors once more.

'The Harvest Festival.'

Shifting, scratching, leg-crossing, coat-repositioning.

'Yes, Mr Iqbal,' said Kate Miniver. 'What about the Harvest Festival?'

'That is precisely what I want to know. What *is* it? *Why* is it? And why must my children celebrate it?'

The headmistress, Mrs Owens, a genteel woman with a soft face half hidden behind a fiercely cut blonde bob, motioned to Katie Miniver that she would handle this.

'Mr Iqbal, we have been through the matter of religious festivals quite thoroughly in the autumn review. As I am sure you are aware, the school already recognises a great variety of religious and secular events: amongst them, Christmas, Ramadan, Chinese New Year, Diwali, Yom Kippur,

Hannukkah, the birthday of Haile Selassie, and the death of Martin Luther King. The Harvest Festival is part of the school's ongoing commitment to religious diversity, Mr Iqbal.'

'I see. And are there many pagans, Mrs Owens, at Manor School?'

'Pagan – I'm afraid I don't under—'

'It is very simple. The Christian calendar has thirty-seven religious events. *Thirty-seven.* The Muslim calendar has *nine.* Only nine. And they are squeezed out by this incredible rash of Christian festivals. Now my motion is simple. If we removed all the pagan festivals from the Christian calendar, there would be an average of' – Samad paused to look at his clipboard – 'of twenty days freed up in which the children could celebrate Lailat-ul-Qadr in December, Eid-ul-Fitr in January and Eid-ul-Adha in April, for example. And the first festival that must go, in my opinion, is this Harvest Festival business.'

'I'm afraid,' said Mrs Owens, doing her pleasant-but-firm smile and playing her punchline to the crowd, 'removing Christian festivals from the face of the earth is a little beyond my jurisdiction. Otherwise I would remove Christmas Eve and save myself a lot of work in stocking-stuffing.'

Samad ignored the general giggle this prompted and pressed on. 'But this is my whole point. This Harvest Festival is *not* a Christian festival. Where in the Bible does it say, *For thou must steal foodstuffs from thy parents' cupboards and bring them into school assembly, and thou shalt force thy mother to bake a loaf of bread in the shape of a fish?* These are pagan ideals! Tell me where does it say, *Thou shalt take a box of frozen fishfingers to an aged crone who lives in Wembley?*'

ZADIE SMITH, *White Teeth* (2000)

BENJAMIN ZEPHANIAH

One of the things that fascinated me as a kid – still fascinates me now – is hypocrisy. There's so much of it. I used to go to one of those Pentecostal churches that are attended by many Caribbean people. I would go along not just on Sunday but also on Monday evening, Wednesday evening and Friday evening. They would be banging tambourines, playing guitars, and beating drums – all very happy clappy, but the preachers there were very fiery. My father was a preacher, but there was another very charismatic preacher – the main performer of what I thought was a big cabaret show. His speciality was preaching about right and wrong, good and evil, and what happens to you when you do good, and what happens to you when you do evil. God was watching you at all times, he would say, and if you did any little bad thing he was going to punish you. He preached about how important it was to live the life and not just preach the words.

Quite often this highly respected preacher drove us home afterwards in a van. As I lived not far from him, he would drop the others off and it would end up with me, and him, and another sister – I don't mean my sister, I mean a sister of the church. He would always lock me in the van when he dropped the sister off, and then he would disappear with her. One day he came back with a smile on his face and I said to him, 'Why do you always go there?' And he said, 'Oh I have to use the bathroom.' After a time I realised what was going on and when he came back to the van once pulling his zip up, I said to him, 'I know what you do. You go there and you kiss her, don't you?'

He pointed his finger at me and said, 'Have respect for your elders.' I said, 'You are being hypocritical,' and he said, 'I am not hypocritical, you are hypocritical because you are not having respect for your elders.' But he knew that I had a point. After that he began to take a slightly different route where I would be dropped off before her!

Sweet hypocrisy. I remember being told by an 'elder' that I should respect my elders and I said, 'Why?' And he said, 'Because they are older.' But I could never understand why I should respect someone just because they happened to be born before me, and I told him so. I also told him that I was a twin, and that I was born fifteen minutes before my sister, but I didn't expect her to respect me just because I was born before her. But he said, 'You must respect your elders.' 'Look,' I said, 'Elders rob, elders cheat, elders make bombs, elders are fighting wars (the Biafran war was raging at the time). Elders are racist, elders damage the earth, and elders do bad things to children, and you want me to respect them because they are older? Hey,' I said, 'Don't take it personally, I don't think all elders do those things, but I can't respect people just because they are older when most of the bad things I have seen in the world are done by elders.' The elder went away scratching his head.

Now is this hypocrisy or what?

It was freezing cold, we were a poor family, and we had no money for the paraffin heaters that we used to heat our houses in them days. Way back then people would also use little paraffin lamps as parking lights next to their parked cars, and there were paraffin lamps in the road like the ones you see at road works today, though I am not sure they are filled with paraffin now. Anyway, my dad drove us in his little Commer van and got us little boys to nick these lamps and empty the paraffin into a big container to take home. We were all very nervous. My dad kept saying, 'Look out, make sure no one's coming.' For some strange reason, when the mission was going well, my brother and I shouted loud, 'The police are coming!' My dad threw the paraffin away, jumped into the van, and drove off. 'We were only joking, Dad,' we said. He went crazy. He took us straight home and gave us a real beating, the type of beating which would get him a life sentence nowadays. And I remember saying to him, 'Dad, why did you beat us?' And he said, 'For lying.' I couldn't believe the hypocrisy, I said, 'Us lying – you were stealing!' And he just slapped me again.

I am from Jamaican parentage. When I was a kid in the playground at school in Birmingham, I didn't just want to play with Jamaican kids. I didn't just want to eat Jamaican food when I went home. I didn't just want to listen to Jamaican music. I loved Irish stuff. I loved Pakistani stuff. I loved Indian stuff. I loved Colombian stuff. When I went home and it was Jamaican food I would say, 'Mum it's all the same, can't we have some Mexican food?' In the playground, I loved kids that came from strange places. I would be asking where they came from and how they dressed. I loved hearing their poetry and their music. I love difference. I thrive on it. I don't want to see the world in black and white, I want to see it in colour, and the world is a colourful place. Our music and poetry reflect that.

Seamus Heaney was spot on when he was asked who was the Bob Dylan of today, who was the poet speaking to young people, and he said, 'Eminem.' It's true because young people think of rap as a form of street poetry. It's a poetry that is relevant to them. The language is raw and sometimes the language upsets elders because it is politically incorrect, but that's how they talk on the streets. Somebody from the Sixties wouldn't have liked some censor saying to them, 'You can't say "reefer"' or 'You can't say "groovy"'. Check this out. I heard Mick Jagger telling his daughter off the other day because the music she was listening to was really loud. Mick Jagger! It's really so easy to forget that you were once young.

Rebellion

'Don't go into Mr MacGregor's garden; your father had an accident there; he was put in a pie by Mrs MacGregor.'

BEATRIX POTTER, *The Tale of Peter Rabbit* (1902)

'If you make me do that,' said Black Sheep very quietly, 'I shall burn this house down and perhaps I *can* kill you – you are so bony, but I will try.'

No punishment followed this blasphemy, though Black Sheep held himself ready to work his way to Auntie Rosa's withered throat and grip there till he was beaten off.

RUDYARD KIPLING, *Baa Baa Black Sheep* in *Wee Willie Winkie and Other Child Stories* (1898)

5 January 1876
You will find as the children grow up that as a rule children are a bitter disappointment – their greatest object being to do precisely what their parents do not wish and have anxiously tried to prevent.

QUEEN VICTORIA, *Queen Victoria in Her Letters & Journals*, ed. Christopher Hibbert (1984)

'I'll show 'em!' he muttered.

And he meant that he would show the world . . . He was honouring the world; he was paying the finest homage to it. In that head of his a flame burnt that was like an altar-fire, a miraculous and beautiful phenomenon, than which nothing is more miraculous nor more beautiful over the whole earth. Whence had it suddenly spring, that flame? After years of muddy inefficiency, of contentedness with the second-rate and the dishonest, that flame astoundingly bursts forth, from a hidden, if unheeded spark that none had ever thought to blow upon . . . Edwin himself seemed no tabernacle for that singular flame. He was not merely untidy and dirty – at his age such defects might have excited in a sane observer uneasiness by their absence; but his gestures and his gait were untidy. He did not mind how he walked. All his sprawling limbs were saying: 'What does it matter, so long as we get there?' The angle of the slatternly bag across his shoulders was an insult to the flame. And yet the flame burned with serene and terrible pureness.

ARNOLD BENNETT, *Clayhanger* (1910)

POSY SIMMONDS

I'm often struck by the way children court disaster. Parental warnings – Don't touch! Be careful! Never, ever do that! Don't go near the edge!' – are almost always incitements for a child to do the opposite, not so much out of disobedience or recklessness, I think it's more to do with curiosity, of testing theory, to see what happens.

But I speak for myself. When we were young, my brothers, my sister and I had all the usual warnings. 'It's extremely dangerous to play with matches.' We understood this theory very well from the story (and the horrid picture) of the child burned to death in *Straw Peter*. We observed real fires. There were open fires in the house, bonfires in the garden and on our farm, and various adults smoked. We understood from sparks, and singeings, and holes in the hearthrug that things could go wrong.

And there we were, my brother and I and our friend Alexa, aged about six and seven. We were in the orchard, as far away from grown-ups as possible, crouching inside an old wooden chicken coop. It was a bit of a squash – the three of us, the straw and the box of Swan Vestas. We took it in turns to strike the matches. That was the best bit – the thrill when the pink bobble burst into flame. We waved the matches around and, when they burned away too much, dropped them in the straw to see what would happen. At first the straw smouldered. Then there were some creeping baby flames and, quite suddenly, big roaring orange ones.

I don't know how we got out unhurt but, miraculously, we did. It was really exciting, the fire and the smoke coming out of the chicken wire, and I remember we whooped and flapped around until the flames found something damp and died down. Then we felt frightened. The half-burnt coop would find us out. We'd get into trouble for playing with matches. (We did.)

'Don't eat sticks,' was another warning. If you did, we were told, you'd get collywobbles and worms and have disgusting medicine and the only way of checking the worms had gone was to use a potty lined with black tissue paper. Of course I ate sticks. Sticks were the weapons allotted to girls and to Little Ones after the Big Ones (my eldest brother and friends) had bagged the pistols and spud guns, and the commanding roles too. 'You're a sentry,' I'd be told, and sent to some remote corner. It was a large garden, planted in the 1880s with lawn, borders, box hedges, yuccas and a wild shrubby bit. It was so boring being a sentry; you peeled the bark off your weapon, examined it, found it white and wormless and you chewed the end till it got soggy. It passed the time.

Posy

293

I never got worms from eating sticks, whereas I frequently got collywobbles from things that were supposed to be good for you – gooseberries, cherries, windfallen apples. It was confusing. You never quite belived what you were told. Being warned something was poisonous was never quite as convincing as touching it with your welly, or holding it and smelling it. *Tasting* it was another matter. I certainly never tasted Deadly Nightshade (the name was so frightening) or laburnum seeds or Lords and Ladies. But pretty little yew berries . . . I remember one cold autumn afternoon making plates out of mud and arranging on them a banquet: bits of box hedge that looked like king cabbages, piles of holly berries and a platter of yew berries mashed to a pink paste. I'm quite, quite sure I licked my fingers. But I can't have. Yew leaves are deadly poisonous, aren't they?

DONNA TARTT

Not long ago, my little godson came to stay with me for the first time: his first summer vacation, and also his first trip to the countryside. Though still an infant, not yet able to speak, his eyes were round and ringing with astonishment all weekend long. Everything at my house was shocking and utterly new: velvet sofa cushions, purple flowers, elderly pug (bigger than he was, a frightening but friendly lion). In the photographs from that weekend (swimming pool; absurd yellow kiddie float) his face is alight with violent wonder – an expression very similar to the dazed, incredulous joy that I remember on the faces of some sombre little hill-children in India at the watermelon sparklers I gave them. These were a racy treat of my American childhood – clear candies of a biting gorgeous pink, deliciously sour, smooth and sparkling like jewels when you took them out of your mouth and held them up to the light after you'd sucked on them for a while. But though they are pretty enough to look at, their taste is the real stunner – an overpowering electric tang to make a grown-up's eyes water, but that children adore. As a child I craved these candies, was driven mad by them, saved my nickels and dimes for them – all the children on my school bus did – but there, in the high Himalaya, they were unheard of, pure magic: I might as well have been handing out rubies.

Of course, it's not at all remarkable that children are captivated by new things, because to children everything is new.

But what is remarkable is how fleeting impressions of child-hood delight can linger and change and vanish and reappear unexpectedly over the years, winking like fireflies throughout the arduous and complicated darks of a lifetime. It has been remarked that a poet's most powerful, passionate metaphors – the ones that recur again and again, the ones that carry the deepest personal meaning – are fixed irrevocably in the mind before the age of twelve. So, too, I think, for the rest of us. Someday, long after I am dead, my little godson may be an old man of eighty or ninety sitting in a deck chair in Miami Beach, inexplicably transfixed with a wordless pang of joy at a striped beach ball, at dazzling turquoise pool water – just as someday (I hope) a particular impossible shade of watermelon pink, glimpsed in passing, may perhaps strike an old lady in a Himalayan hill-village as the very sweetness of youth.

Quite often there's a pattern to these haphazard and apparently random flashes of childhood memory – a pattern which doesn't emerge or make itself known until later in life. One particularly vivid memory that has stayed with me throughout my life, and will be with me until I die, is of the first time I saw a hummingbird. The incident was inconsequential enough; I was about four years old, and had accompanied my beloved great-grandmother (then in her late seventies) to a garden party given for a distant relative: a young bride-to-be. It was springtime: the azaleas were in spectacular bloom; the astonishing little ruby-throated creature flew right in front of me – down at my eye level, practically in front of my face – and hovered there for some moments before it buzzed forward, then backward, then flew away across the green lawn for ever.

That was all. It can have lasted no more than ten seconds, yet this tiny incident has left a much more intense and lasting impression on me than many of the great landmark events of my childhood. For many years, I wondered exactly why I remembered this specific incident so vividly and not something else, something more powerful. Why the hummingbird? What was it trying to tell me? Why had this memory, and not some other, struck me so forcefully in the first place; why does it come back to me so persistently, in memory and in dream?

Only now – at mid-life, in my fortieth year – am I starting to realize what the hummingbird means, and why – at unexpected moments – it returns to me still. It is a premonition of Heaven, and of Death. My great-grandmother (who was leaning beside me, holding my hand, as the hummingbird paused in mid-air before me) did not have long to live. Nor did the bride herself – lovely laughing Ginger, who died young, of cancer. I couldn't have understood it then, and scarcely understand it now, but my entire subsequent impressions of death, and beauty, and mutability, and the brevity of life itself are somehow crystallised perfectly in those few moments, when the tiny iridescent hummingbird darted before my face, hovered briefly, then flew away. All I know of the sublime is somehow encapsulated and encoded in that instant: flowers everywhere, white-gloved ladies in pastel dresses. Then beautiful Ginger, in an apple-green dress, kneeling to say hello.

The Land of Lost Content

All children, except one, grow up.

J. M. BARRIE, *Peter Pan* (1911)

But then, thought Alice, shall I never get any older than I am now? That'll be a comfort, one way – never to be an old woman – but then – always to have lessons to learn! Oh I shouldn't like that!

LEWIS CARROLL, *Alice's Adventures in Wonderland* (1871)

Any life you look at seems unhappy but any life lived is fairly cheerful, and whatever happens goes on being so.

I remember being so surprised when I was little girl reading what I had written as my thoughts, they were very awful thoughts but naturally I had a good time then as I have had a good time since.

GERTRUDE STEIN, *Everybody's Autobiography* (1937)

What are those blue remembered hills,
What spires, what farms are those?

That is the land of lost content,
I see it shining plain,
The happy highways where I went
And cannot come again.

A. E. HOUSMAN, *A Shropshire Lad* (1896)

ACKNOWLEDGEMENTS

For permission to reprint copyright material the publishers gratefully acknowledge the following: A.E.B examination questions are reproduced by permission of the Assessment and Qualifications Alliance. KINGSLEY AMIS, from *Memoirs* by Kingsley Amis, published by Hutchinson. Copyright © Kingsley Amis 1991. Reprinted by permission of The Random House Group Ltd. and by kind permission of Jonathan Clowes Ltd., on behalf of the Literary Estate of Sir Kingsley Amis. MARTIN AMIS, from *Experience* published by Jonathan Cape, reproduced by permission of The Wylie Agency. MAYA ANGELOU, extracts from *I Know Why the Caged Bird Sings*, reproduced by kind permission of Virago Press, a division of Time Warner Book Group UK and Random House Inc., US. DIANA ATHILL, from *Yesterday Morning*, reproduced by permission of Granta Books. B.B., from *Brendan Chase* copyright © D.J. Watkins-Pitchford 1944, published by Ernest Benn (Re-issued Jane Nissen Books 2000.) Extract from *A Child Alone* copyright © D.J. Watkins-Pitchford 1978, published by Michael Joseph 1978, reproduced by permission of David Higham Associates. J.M. BARRIE, extract from *Peter Pan and Wendy* reproduced by kind permission of Great Ormond Street Hospital Children's Charity © 1937. H. E. BATES from *The Vanished World*, Vol. I, copyright © H. E. Bates 1969, published by Michael Joseph. Reproduced by permission of Pollinger Limited and the proprietor. NINA BAWDEN, from *Carrie's War* copyright © Nina Bawden, 1973, reproduced by permission of Curtis Brown on behalf of Nina Bawden. Excerpt from *In My Own Time: Almost an Autobiography* by Nina Bawden. Text copyright © 1994 by Nina Bawden. Reprinted by permission of Clarion Books/Houghton Mifflin Company and Virago Press, a division of Time Warner Book Group UK. All rights reserved. ALAN BENNETT, from *Forty Years On*, copyright © Alan Bennett 1969, published by Faber & Faber Ltd. 1969. *Writing Home*, copyright © Alan Bennett 1994, published by Faber & Faber Ltd., 1994 reprinted by permission of Faber & Faber Ltd. ARNOLD BENNETT, from *Clayhanger*, (Methuen 1910) and from *The Truth About an Author*, (Constable 1903), by permission of A. P. Watt Ltd. on behalf of Jacques Eldin. JOHN BETJEMAN extract from letter by John Betjeman from *Evening Standard* (25 August 1934) by permission of the Estate of Sir John Betjeman. MAEVE BINCHY, from *Not like mother used to make thank heaven* printed in the *Guardian* 29 October 2003, copyright © Maeve Binchy 2003. Reprinted by permission of the *Guardian*. ENID BLYTON, from *Five on a Treasure Island*, reproduced with the kind permission of Enid Blyton Ltd. Copyright © 1942 Enid Blyton Ltd., a Chorion company. All rights reserved. DIRK BOGARDE, from *A Postillion Struck By Lightning*, published by Chatto & Windus. Reprinted by permission of The Random House Group Ltd. JOHN BUCHAN, from *Memory Hold-the-Door* published by Bodley Head 1964, copyright © A. P. Watt Ltd. Reprinted by permission of A. P. Watt Ltd. on behalf of The Lord

Tweedsmuir and Jean, Lady Tweedsmuir. JOANNA BRISCOE, from 'Parents: too much too young', the *Guardian* 18 June 2003, reproduced by permnission of the author. HENRI CARTIER-BRESSON, from *Le Monde,* 23 August 2002 reprinted by permission of *Le Monde.* JUNG CHANG, from *Wild Swans,* (Harper Collins 1991). Copyright © Jung Chang 1991. Copyright © 1991 by Globalflair Ltd. Reprinted by permission of HarperCollins Publishers Ltd. CHARLES CHAPLIN, from *My Autobiography* by Charles Chaplin, published by Bodley Head. Reprinted by permission of the Random House Group Ltd. Copyright © Bodley Head 1964. G. K. CHESTERTON, from *Autobiography,* (Hutchinson 1936) by permission of A.P.Watt Ltd. on behalf of The Royal Literary Fund. AGATHA CHRISTIE, from *Autobiography,* copyright © Agatha Christie 1977, reproduced by permission of HarperCollins Publishers Ltd.. WINSTON CHURCHILL, from *My Early Life,* © Winston S. Churchill, reproduced by permission of Curtis Brown on behalf of the estate of Winston S. Churchill. RICHMAL CROMPTON, from *William in Trouble* published by George Newnes (1927), reproduced by permission of A. P.Watt Ltd. on behalf of Richmal Ashbee. ROALD DAHL, from *Boy,* published by Jonathan Cape Ltd. Reproduced by permission of David Higham Associates. ALAN DAVIDSON, selection under 'T': Tapioca, extract from *The Oxford Companion to Food,* edited by Alan Davidson (1999), by permission of Oxford University Press. ANGELICA GARNETT, from *Deceived with Kindness,* published by Chatto & Windus. Reprinted by permission of The Random House Group Ltd. EVE GARNETT, from *The Family from One End Street,* by permission of Gregory & Co Agents, on behalf of The Estate of Eve Garnett. ROBERT GRAVES, from *Goodbye to All That,* published by Jonathan Cape 1929. Reproduced by permission of Carcanet Press Ltd. GRAHAM GREENE, from *A Sort of Life,* (Bodley Head 1971) and from 'The Lost Childhood' in *Collected Essays,* published by Bodley Head 1969, by permission of David Higham Associates. GERMAINE GREER, from *Daddy We Hardly Knew You* (Hamish Hamilton 1989). Copyright © Germaine Greer. Reprinted by permission of the author. WALTER GREENWOOD, from *The Old School,* Ed. Graham Greene, published by Jonathan Cape 1934, by permission of Nicholas Evans. ALEC GUINNESS, from *Blessings in Disguise* (Hamish Hamilton 1996). Copyright © Sir Alec Guinness, 1996. Reproduced by permission of Penguin Books Ltd. L. P. HARTLEY, from *The Go-Between* (Hamish Hamilton, 1953). Copyright © L. P. Hartley 1953. This edition copyright © Douglas Brook-Douglas, 1997. Reproduced by permission of The Society of Authors as the Literary Representative of the Estate of L. P. Hartley. and Penguin Books Ltd. BARBARA HEPWORTH, from *A Pictorial Biography* published by Adams & Dart 1970, copyright © Bowness, Hepworth Estate, by permission of Alan Bowness. BARRY HINES, from *A Kestrel For A Knave* (Michael Joseph 1968). Copyright © Barry Hines, 1968. Reproduced by permission of Penguin Books Ltd. and by permission of The Agency (London) Ltd. All rights reserved and enquiries to The Agency (London) Ltd., 24 Pottery Lane, London W11 4LZ, fax: 0207 727 9037. SIMON HOGGART *Fixed smiles greet the sex revelations of Sarah,* printed in the *Guardian* 29 October 2003, copyright © The *Guardian* 2003. Reprinted by permission of the *Guardian.* HOMER, *The Iliad of Homer,* trs. by Richard Latimore copyright © University of Chicago 1951, published by University of Chicago Press 1951., by permission of the University of Chicago Press. BOB HOPE, from *My Life in Jokes,* by Bob Hope. Copyright © 2003 Bob Hope. Reprinted by permission of Hyperion. NICK HORNBY, from *Fever Pitch* copyright © Nick Hornby 1992, published by Victor

What is UNICEF?

UNICEF, the United Nations Children's Fund, is the world's largest development organisation working specifically for children and children's rights. The UN Convention on the Rights of the Child underpins all of our work, with the overarching goal of promoting dignity, security and self-fulfilment for all children, everywhere.

What we do

UNICEF believes that nurturing and caring for children are the cornerstones of human progress. We work with local communities, organisations and governments in 157 countries across the globe to advocate for children's rights, to help meet their basic needs and to expand their opportunities to reach their full potential. This is achieved through long-term development programmes in health care and education, for example, as well as emergency work in times of crisis.

In developed countries, the organisation plays a leading role in changing attitudes and winning support for children's rights by campaigning on UK and international children's issues, working with partners in local organisations, schools, hospitals and business, and raising money to support UNICEF's programmes internationally.

To find out more about UNICEF and how you can support us, please visit *www.unicef.org.uk*

NOTES ON CONTRIBUTORS

KOFI ANNAN *b.* 1938, Ghana. Educated University of Science and Technology, Kumasi, Ghana; Macalester College, St. Paul, Minnesota; Institut des Hautes Études Internationales, Geneva. Secretary-General, United Nations since 1997. Various posts in the UN and WHO. Nobel Peace Prize 1991.

JEFFREY ARCHER *b.* 1940, Somerset. Educated Brasenose College, Oxford. Athletics Blues. Writer and politician. MP (C) Louth 1969–1976. Deputy Chairman Con. Party 1985–86. Several novels. Most recent books: *A Prison Diary*, *Sons of Fortune*. Life Peer 1992.

CORNELIA BATHURST *b.* North Lanarkshire, last of large family. Boarding school in Hertfordshire for 8 years (by train). Photographer. Lives in London and Scotland and, at least partly, on the A1. Three daughters and assorted livestock.

KATHLEEN CASSIDY *b.* 1927, Felling-on-Tyne. Educated St John's School, St Patrick's School. Tea Lady at St James Newcastle United Football Club. Has brewed tea for 14 managers in her time, including Kevin Keegan and Bobby Robson. Lives in Wallsend.

JUNG CHANG *b.* 1952, Yibin, People's Republic of China. Educated Sichuan University, York University. Writer and lecturer. Worked as farm labourer, 'barefoot doctor', steelworker and electrician. Left China for Britain in 1978. Memoir: *Wild Swans*, *Three Daughters of China*. Lives in London.

BRIAN COX *b.* 1946, Dundee. Educated poorly, then LAMDA. Actor/writer/teacher/director. Appeared in many theatres over 40 years. Films include: *Troy, X Men 2, Adaptation, Manhunter,* etc. Awards: Two Oliviers, Emmy, Lucille Lortel. Publications: *Salem to Moscow, The Lear Diaries.*

SOPHIE DAHL *b.* 1977, London. Educated Bedales and King Alfred School. International model and writer. Granddaughter of Roald Dahl. Novella: *The Man With the Dancing Eyes.* Currently working on a novel. Lives in New York.

BILL DE QUICK *b.* 1945, Plymouth. Educated Oakmeads, Burgess Hill. Runs his own printing company. Server at Little St Mary's Church, Cambridge. Eventually traced his father's family in USA. Lives in Cambridge.

JOSSLYN GORE-BOOTH *b.* 1950, Raby Castle, Co. Durham. Educated Eton, Balliol College, Oxford, and INSEAD. Sometime economist, banker, management consultant, and custodian, until 2004, of Lissadell, Co. Sligo. Now living in Durham.

YORAM GROSS *b.* 1926, Poland. Educated Krakow University. Producer/director/scriptwriter. Heads Australia's most successful animation production house. His films have won numerous awards, and the hearts and minds of children worldwide. Awarded the prestigious Order of Australia in 1995. Lives in Sydney with his family.

ROGER HANCOCK *b.* 1931, Bournemouth, Hants. Educated at Tonbridge School and Loomis Institute, Connecticut, USA. Chairman of literary agency, Roger Hancock Ltd. Lives in Brighton with an old blonde.

SEAMUS HEANEY *b.* 1939, Northern Ireland. Educated St Columb's College, Derry, and Queen's University, Belfast. Poet and translator. Recent work includes *Opened Ground: Poems 1966–1996; Beowulf, A New Verse Translation; Finders Keepers: Selected Prose 1971–2001,* and *Electric Light.* Lives in Dublin.

PATRICIA HODGE *b.* 1946, Lincolnshire. Educated Wintringham Grammar School, Grimsby, St. Helen's School, Northwood, LAMDA. Hon. D.Litt. Hull, Brunel, Leicester. Actress. Many appearances in TV, film, theatre. Six award nominations; Olivier Award 2000 for *Money*, National Theatre. Lives in London.

ROLF INHAUSER *b.* 1939, Steinhöring, Germany. Essayist, radio and television journalist in Germany, followed by a 30-year stint as senior editor of a children's book publishing house in Switzerland. Currently, he is living out his retirement in Paris.

PENELOPE LIVELY *b.* 1933, Egypt. Educated St Anne's College, Oxford. Writer. Publications include: *The Ghost of Thomas Kempe* (for children), *Moon Tiger* (for adults), *Oleander, Jacaranda: a childhood perceived* (memoir). Lives in London but flees to Somerset when possible, and writes anywhere.

PATRICIA McARTHUR *b.* 1945, Chester. Educated Dee House Convent School and St Paul's Teacher Training college, Rugby. Primary school teacher. Living happily on edge of Llandegla Moors, North Wales, with a collection of chickens, old dog, horse and moped.

MARINA MAHLER *b.* 1 August, London. Age? Old and young. Education? Life itself, not much else. Founder: The International Gustav Mahler Foundation (Amsterdam). After absorbing the family ghosts, I manage to ease slowly into my own music. Resulting activities begin to flower. Lives in Italy.

JOHN MAJOR *b.* 1943, Surrey. Educated: Rutlish Grammar School. Politician (Conservative Party) and banker. Served in Government for 16 years, 10 of them in Cabinet, including Foreign and Commonwealth Secretary 1989, Chancellor of the Exchequer 1989-90, Prime Minister 1990-97, CH 1999. President of Surrey County Cricket Club at the Oval 2000-02. Autobiography: *John Major: The Autobiography.*

TOM MASCHLER *b.* 1933, Berlin. Educated Leighton Park School. Publisher. André Deutsch, MacGibbon & Kee, Penguin, Jonathan Cape (Chairman). Assoc. Producer *The French Lieutenant's Woman* (film). Publications (Editor): *Declarations* and *New English Dramatists* series. Lives in France and London.

DEBORAH MOGGACH *b.* 1948, London. Educated Camden School for Girls, Bristol University. Writer. Her 15 novels include *Tulip Fever* and the latest, *These Foolish Things*. She grew up with three sisters, and spent a lot of her childhood in the New Forest. Lives in London.

ANDREW O'HAGAN *b.* 1968, Glasgow. Educated University of Strathclyde. Novelist and essayist. Publications include: *The Missing, Our Fathers, Personality*. He now has a baby daughter, Nell, who swims through his dreams every night. Lives in London.

ONORA O'NEILL *b.* 1941, Aughafatten, NI. Educated St Paul's Girls' School, Oxford, Harvard. Principal, Newnham College, Cambridge. Writes on political philosophy and ethics. Books: *Towards Justice and Virtue*; *Bounds of Justice, Autonomy and Trust in Bioethics; A Question of Trust*. Life Peer 1999.

MICHAEL PALIN *b.* 1943, Sheffield. Educated Brasenose College, Oxford. Actor/writer/traveller. Works include: *Monty Python's Flying Circus, Ripping Yarns*, 6 BBC travel series, the films *Time Bandits, The Missionary, A Private Function, A Fish Called Wanda, American Friends* and a novel, *Hemingway's Chair*. Lives in London.

JAN PIEŃKOWSKI *b.* 1936, Warsaw. Educated King's College, Cambridge. Author and designer: graphic, surface and stage. Books include: *Haunted House, Dinner Time* and other pop-up titles; *The Kingdom Under the Sea* and other silhouette books and the *Meg and Mog* series. Lives in Barnes.

TIM PIGOTT-SMITH *b.* 1946, Rugby. Educated Bristol University, Bristol Old Vic Theatre School. Actor. Has played leading roles with the Royal Shakespeare Company, the Royal National Theatre, in the West End, and on Broadway. Many appearances on TV, and has filmed all over the world.

MAURICE SENDAK *b.* 1928, Brooklyn, New York. Author and illustrator. Publications include: *Where the Wild Things Are, In the Night Kitchen, Outside Over There, We Are All In The Dumps With Jack and Guy, I saw Esau,* and *Brundibar.* Lives in Connecticut.

RT. REVD. DAVID SHEPPARD *b.* 1929, Barbados. Educated Trinity Hall, Cambridge. Bishop of Liverpool 1975–1997. Cricket: Played 22 times for England 1950–1963. Captain 1954. President Sussex CCC 2001–02. Autobiography: *Steps Along Hope Street.* Life Peer 1998.

POSY SIMMONDS *b.* 1945, Maidenhead, Berkshire. Educated Queen Ann's School, Caversham, Central School of Art & Design. Cartoonist and writer. Cartoons include 'Literary Life' for the *Guardian.* Publications include: *Gemma Bovery, Mrs Weber's Diary, Fred.* Married and lives in London.

SYLVIA SYMS *b.* 1934, London. Educated at 6 schools, finally Selshurst Grammar, then RADA, graduating 1953. Actress/director/producer. Over 40 films including *Ice Cold in Alex,* and 60 appearances in theatre, TV, radio, etc. Several awards.

DONNA TARTT *b.* 1963, Greenwood, Mississippi. Educated Bennington College, University of Mississippi. Writer. Novels include: *The Secret History, The Little Friend.* Lives in Virginia and New York City.

ALEXANDER THYNN *b.* 1932. 7th Marquess of Bath (and formerly Viscount Weymouth). Educated at Eton and Oxford. His extensive murals are on display at Longleat House, while his vast autobiography, *Strictly Private,* includes all 4 of his novels and his poetry. See www.lordbath.co.uk.

BENJAMIN ZEPHANIAH *b.* 1958, Birmingham. Educated Broadway Comprehensive and Boreatton Park School. Writer. Publications include: *Talking Turkeys, Funky Chickens, Face, Refugee Boy, Gangsta Rap.* Lives in East London.

INDEX

Alcott, Louisa M. 271
Amis, Kingsley 153
Amis, Martin 161–2
Angelou, Maya 143, 184
Annan, Kofi, 19
Archer, Jeffrey 116–7
Associated Examining Board 15–16
Atherton, Elizabeth 115
Athill, Diana 182–3
Atwood, Margaret 131
B., B. 224
Barrie, J. M. 298
Barton, Dick 198
Bates, H. E. 279–80
Bathurst, Cornelia 212–220
Bawden, Nina 237
Bennett, Alan 113, 149–50, 208–9
Bennett, Arnold 27, 207, 291
Betjeman, John 182
Binchy, Maeve 55
Blyton, Enid 208
Bogarde, Dirk 17, 112, 144
Briscoe, Joanna 72
Buchan, John 91
Carroll, Lewis 14, 134, 168, 298
Cartier-Bresson, Henri 25
Cassidy, Kathleen 173–81
Chang, Jung 47–49, 52
Chaplin, Charles 51
Chesterton, G. K. 26, 71
Christie, Agatha 4, 73, 89
Churchill, Winston 5, 20
Cobbett, William 119
Cohen, Gerry 162
Cox, Brian 201–4
Crompton, Richmal 221

Cutler, Ivor 168
Dahl, Roald 35–6
Dahl, Sophie 154–6
Davidson, Alan 56
De Quick, Bill 258–68
Dickens, Charles 5–6, 17, 135, 184
Eliot, George 183
Evans, Peter 114
Garnett, Angelica 222
Garnett, Eve 207–8
Gaskell, James Milnes 28–31
Godwin, William 279
Gore-Booth, Josslyn 94–105
Grahame, Kenneth 57
Graves, Robert 46
Greene, Graham 4, 130, 205
Greenwood, Walter 18
Greer, Germaine 157, 211
Gross, Yoram 233–6
Guinness, Alec 66–9
Hancock, Roger 240–1
Harris, Dave 162
Hartley, L. P. 82, 160
Heaney, Seamus 11
Hepworth, Barbara 33
Hines, Barry 210
Hodge, Patricia 7-8
Hodgson-Burnett, Frances 89, 222
Hoffman, Dr Heinrich 272
Hoggart, Simon 151–2
Homer 128
Hope, Bob 182
Hornby, Nick 85
Housman, A. E. 299
Inhauser, Rolf 242–50
Jeal, Tim 159